S0-BWP-939

· 1 ·

A Hermeneutic of Curiosity and Readings of Psalm 61

תורא נביאים כתובים

STUDIES IN OLD TESTAMENT INTERPRETATION

Series editors
Jeffrey S. Rogers, Furman University
Cecil P. Staton, Jr., Mercer University

1. *A Hermeneutic of Curiosity and Readings of Psalm 61* (1995)

תורא נביאים כתובים

תורא נביאים כתובים

STUDIES IN OLD TESTAMENT INTERPRETATION

·1·

A Hermeneutic of Curiosity and Readings of Psalm 61

❏

W. H. Bellinger, Jr.

❏

MERCER UNIVERSITY PRESS
·1995·

Hiebert Library
Fresno Pacific College - M. B. Seminary
Fresno, CA 93702

ISBN 0-86554-464-6   MUP/H364

A Hermeneutic of Curiosity and Readings of Psalm 61
Copyright ©1995
Mercer University Press, Macon, Georgia 31210-3960 USA
All rights reserved
Printed in the United States of America

❏

The paper used in this publication meets the minimum
requirements of American National Standard
for Information Sciences—Permanence of Paper
for Printed Library Materials, ANSI Z39.48–1984.

❏

Library of Congress Cataloging-in-Publication Data

A hermeneutic of curiosity and readings of Psalm 61
by W. H. Bellinger, Jr.
ISBN 0-86554-464-6
viii+152 pp. 6x9" (15x23cm.).

A catalog record for this book
is available from the Library of Congress.

Contents

Preface

Much of the work for this monograph was accomplished during a sabbatical leave in 1989 at Fitzwilliam College in the University of Cambridge. I am grateful to Baylor University for that opportunity. I am also grateful to Baylor, its administrators, and its faculty for a context in which to pursue my work. This study was supported in part by funds from the Baylor University Research Committee. The work was also supported by the Centennial Class of Baylor University with its Centennial Professor Fund. While I was in Cambridge, I enjoyed the status of Visiting Scholar at Fitzwilliam College. I am grateful to Dr. Graham I. Davies for that privilege.

The production of a monograph owes much to many. I have indicated my debt to many scholars. Several individuals have offered special assistance: Tony Moyers, Ronald Clements, Mikeal Parsons, and Roy Melugin. My graduate assistant Walter Crouch has given invaluable help. My wife Libby and children Jill and Chip have supported my scholarly endeavors; Libby has also helped in the editorial process. I am especially grateful to Dr. Cecil P. Staton, Jr., of Mercer University Press and Dr. Jeffrey S. Rogers of Furman University for including this monograph in the series Studies in Old Testament Interpretation.

Much of the thought and passion of my professional life relates to questions of biblical hermeneutics and method in psalm studies. I was educated in the historical-critical approach, primarily in form criticism and biblical theology. This study illustrates my attempts at moving forward to include more contemporary approaches. It is my sincerest wish that this volume contribute to our conversation on such interpretive issues.

June 1994   *W. H. Bellinger, Jr.*

Abbreviations

AB	Anchor Bible	LSCB	Lutterworth Studies
ASOR	American Schools of Oriental Research		in Church and Bible
BDB	Brown, Driver, and Briggs, *Hebrew*	NCB	New Century Bible
	and English Lexicon of the Old Testament	IBT	Overtures to Biblical Theology
BHS	*Biblia Hebraica Stuttgartensia*	OTL	Old Testament Library
BibS(N)	Biblische Studien (Neukirchen)	OTM	Old Testament Message
BJRL	*Bulletin of the John Rylands*	OBO	Orbis biblicus et orientalis
	University Library of Manchester	PTMS	Pittsburgh Theological
BZ	*Biblische Zeitschrift*		Monograph Series
CBC	Cambridge Bible Commentary	SBL	Society of Biblical Literature
CBQ	*Catholic Biblical Quarterly*	SBLDS	SBL Dissertation Series
CBSC	Cambridge Bible for Schools and Colleges	SBLSP	SBL Seminar Papers
CThM	Calwer Theologische Monographien	SBS	Stuttgarter Bibelstudien
FOTL	The Forms of Old Testament Literature	SBT	Studies in Biblical Theology
GBS	Guides to Biblical Scholarship	*StTh*	*Studia Theologica*
GHK	Handkommentar zum Alten Testament	TBC	Torch Bible Commentaries
GKC	Gesenius's Hebrew Grammar,	*TDNT*	*Theological Dictionary*
	ed. E. Kautzsch, trans. A. E. Cowley		*of the New Testament*
H	Hebrew versification (Masoretic text)	*TDOT*	*Theological Dictionary*
HAR	*Hebrew Annual Review*		*of the Old Testament*
HAT	Handbuch zum Alten Testament	*TGUOS*	*Transactions of the Glasgow*
HBT	*Horizons in Biblical Theology*		*University Oriental Society*
HSM	Harvard Semitic Monographs	*THAT*	*Theologisches Handwörterbuch*
HUCA	*Hebrew Union College Annual*		*zum Alten Testament*
IB	*Interpreter's Bible*	*TWAT*	*Theologisches Wörterbuch*
IDB	*Interpreter's Dictionary of the Bible*		*zum Alten Testament*
Int	*Interpretation*	*TynBul*	*Tyndale Bulletin*
IRT	Issues in Religion and Theology	*USQR*	*Union Seminary*
JANES	*Journal of the Ancient Near Eastern*		*Quarterly Review*
	Society of Columbia University	*VT*	*Vetus Testamentum*
JBL	*Journal of Biblical Literature*	VTSup	VT supplements
JR	*Journal of Religion*	WBC	Word Biblical Commentary
JSNTSup	Journal for the Study of the New	WC	Westminster Commentaries
	Testament supplement series	WMANT	Wissenschaftliche Monographie
JSOT	*Journal for the Study of the Old Testament*		zum Alten und Neuen Testament
JSOTSup	JSOT supplement series	*ZAW*	*Zeitschrift für die*
JSS	*Journal of Semitic Studies*		*alttestamentliche Wissenschaft*

A Framework

The Issue

The hermeneutical debate rages intensely in biblical studies today. The debate has come to the fore because of doubts cast upon what has become, in academic circles, the traditional historical-critical model for practicing biblical interpretation. Consider two sides to the debate; first note those who challenge the historical model:

> I believe attempts to maintain or redefine the historical method are doomed to failure because the historical method of criticism is no longer the prevailing method. We can no longer equate meaning with what the text meant and take what the text meant as the result, pure and simple, of its historical and cultural context.[1]

That quote from Edgar McKnight reflects a tone similar to that of Meir Sternberg in his influential volume on biblical narrative. While Sternberg would not deny the value of historical inquiry, his attack on the "geneticist" approach to biblical interpretation at times carries more sting than McKnight's.

> Insiders need no telling that such idle speculation passes for scholarship in biblical circles, where it has long occupied a place of honor. (The very term "higher criticism" was coined, in J. G. Eichhorn's *Einleitung in das Alte Testament* (1780-83), to distinguish and promote the inquiry into questions of authorship.) Indeed, this exercise in futility is worth lingering over only because it dramatizes a traditional will-o'-the-wisp of source criticism. I have in mind the focus on the real writer (or writership) as a historical figure (or process) at the expense of the

---

[1]Edgar V. McKnight, *The Bible and the Reader: An Introduction to Literary Criticism* (Philadelphia: Fortress Press, 1985) xvi.

author or narrator as an artistic persona, or, worse, the confusion of the two.[2]

Or note Sternberg's comments earlier in the volume.

> Source-oriented critics often imply that they deal in hard facts and consign "aesthetic" analysis to its fate at the none too reliable hands of the literary coterie. If seriously entertained, this is a delusion, bearing the name of positivism with none of its excuses and facilities. There is simply nothing here to be positive about—no, or almost no, facts concerning the sources of the Bible apart from those we ourselves make by inference from the Bible as source.[3]

In other words, "In their concern with whatever frames or antecedes the text, the historians tend to overlook the chief body of historical evidence that awaits proper interpretation."[4]

Contrast such a view with the statement of James Smart: "Everything in Scripture is history and must be open to the most thoroughly critical and reconstructive investigation."[5] Smart insists that biblical interpretion be theological as well as historical, but he makes it clear that the historical-critical approach is essential for proper interpretation. While James Barr offers his own critique of many traditional biblical investigations, he would agree with Smart that the search for historical context is essential to the task of interpretation.[6] Note also the ever-growing number of source-critical studies on the Pentateuch, all of which assume that historical investigation is the key to interpretation.[7]

---

[2]Meir Sternberg, *The Poetics of Biblical Narrative: Ideological Literature and the Drama of Reading*, Indiana Studies in Biblical Literature (Bloomington: Indiana University Press, 1985) 64.

[3]Ibid., 16.

[4]Ibid., 11.

[5]James D. Smart, *The Past, Present, and Future of Biblical Theology* (Philadelphia: Westminster Press, 1979) 145.

[6]See James Barr, *The Bible in the Modern World* (London: SCM Press, 1973). Historical concerns pervade the book.

[7]See, for example, Werner H. Schmidt, *Old Testament Introduction*, trans. Matthew J. O'Connell (New York: Crossroad, 1984) 41-135; Lloyd M. Barre, "The Riddle of the Flood Chronology," *JSOT* 41 (1988): 3-20.

David Gunn has recently written that the historical-critical approach and newer literary approaches are so different as to be mutually exclusive.[8] They have different goals. The debate rages between those who would stay with the historical-critical approach as normative for biblical interpreters and those who would argue for the priority of an approach more in line with recent hermeneutical theories, text-immanent or reader-oriented approaches.

The broader question is how we are to read/interpret texts. What is the proper starting point? Much of the debate has centered on whether the interpreter's starting point is to be historical or otherwise, but the real issue has to do with one's hermeneutical approach to texts. How do we make sense out of what we read? That question dominates much of American biblical scholarship. In my sixteen years of teaching Old Testament, the discipline of biblical studies has been in turmoil over questions of method. At the annual meetings of the Society of Biblical Literature, much of the talk has focused on how we are to read the Bible. How can we understand or meaningfully read biblical texts? What methods are we to use? The professional guild is still in something of a quandary about such questions, but the contour of the options available has taken on some clarity. A number of scholars insist that we continue to read the Bible by way of the traditional historical-critical approach. Others call us to move beyond such an approach to one more in tune with recent literary and philosophical studies. I intend to converse with the voices of the current debate as I make a proposal that may help to move the discussion forward.

A Proposal

To provide a way forward, let me propose a model for interpretation which is in line with recent developments in literary criticism.

Aspects of Interpretation. When interpreters come to read a biblical text, three aspects come into play: "author," text, reader.[9] First of all,

---

[8]David M. Gunn, "New Directions in the Study of Biblical Hebrew Narrative," *JSOT* 39 (1987): 73.

[9]Compare Norman Perrin, "Historical Criticism, Literary Criticism and Hermeneutics," *JR* 52 (1972): 362-64. W. Randolph Tate, *Biblical Interpretation: An Integrated Approach* (Peabody MA: Hendrickson, 1991) speaks of the world

texts, biblical texts, come from somewhere; there was a point of origin.[10] There was an author or authors of some description, and the text does reflect a history. Many biblical texts speak of historical settings, but all of them originated from a cultural or socio-historical background of some sort. They came about by way of a process, however short, in a historical setting. Such issues we may label with the term "origin." The author may have been central, but there are broader issues related to origins.

Second, there is the text itself, an essential phenomenon for the interpretive task. It betrays a shape and uses language in identifiable ways. Much of the hermeneutical task relates to the content and form of the text. The text is, after all, the object of interpretation and so it is only reasonable that it take a large portion of the attention of the reader.

Third, there is the reader. The reader is the interpreter and here the hermeneutical task comes to fruition. Readers bring concerns to the text and perform certain tasks when reading; the reading process has an appreciable impact on interpretation. Without attention to the reader, one is left in the past or with a text in the abstract. The great diversity of interpretations of texts show the impact of readers on the hermeneutical task.

We could represent these three aspects of interpretation as follows.

TEXT

ORIGIN   READER

Methodology. When we explore issues related to origin, we use methods designed to look for historical setting, form, source, or textual history. From where did the text originate? The method here is that of the traditional historical-critical approach. Textual criticism probably fits here because it centers on history. Source, form, and redaction criticism are at the center of this concern. They trace the composition history of a text. Tradition history and perhaps even canonical criticism also fit here. As recent hermeneutical discussion has revealed, there are limits upon the

---

behind the text, within the text, and in front of the text.

[10]See Paul Ricoeur, *Interpretation Theory: Discourse and the Surplus of Meaning* (Fort Worth: Texas Christian University Press, 1976) 30.

knowledge we can gain from these historical investigations. However, to ignore questions of history is to deny that a text has a history, to deny what I would suggest is self-evident. Our conclusions about questions of origin need to be tentative and our knowledge may well be limited, but my view is that we would lose a great deal if we did not ask the historical-critical questions. Such investigation does not settle the interpretive dilemma; it is not the nadir of reading. At the same time, we learn a lot about the text and about interpretation in historical-critical investigation.

When we focus on the text itself, we ask questions about the rhetoric, plot, narrative or poetic structure of the text. More formal analyses fit here. Rhetorical criticism, New Critical work and perhaps even the work of structuralists come to the fore in such textual analyses. Again, these investigations alone do not complete the interpretive task; but they are at its heart for they focus on the phenomenon of the text, which is what brought us to the task of reading in the first place.

When we come to the reader, we explore the shape of the process of reading and the context of the reader and any implications of the relation between text and reader. The context of the reader must be noted as an influence on the task of interpretation. The various dimensions of the process of reading are also important. The varieties of reader-response criticism deal with this aspect of interpretation.

According to this schema, then, when we consider the various aspects of the interpretive task and the methodological implications, we find ourselves in a situation of methodological pluralism.[11]

Implications. This methodological pluralism relates to the generation of a multiplicity of readings. The practice of textual criticism produces

---

[11]John Barton, *Reading the Old Testament: Method in Biblical Study* (Philadelphia: Westminster Press, 1984) has provided a valuable treatment of method in biblical study. He suggests that rather than looking for the "right" method, we explore the purpose of the various methods and how they might inform the reader. See also Steven L. McKenzie and Stephen R. Haynes, eds., *To Each Its Own Meaning: An Introduction to Biblical Criticisms and Their Application* (Louisville: Westminster/John Knox Press, 1993); J. Cheryl Exum and David J. A. Clines, eds., *The New Literary Criticism and the Hebrew Bible*, JSOTSup 143 (Sheffield: JSOT Press, 1993); and Paul R. House, *Beyond Form Criticism: Essays in Old Testament Literary Criticism* (Winona Lake IN: Eisenbrauns, 1992).

a kind of reading. The use of form criticism and the use of canonical criticism lead to different nuances in interpreting texts. The use of more text-immanent methods, such as rhetorical analysis, brings yet other dimensions in reading a text. Reader-response criticism will produce additional readings of texts.

Such an approach resonates with the aspects of interpretation I noted above. It also fits my understanding of texts and interpretation. Texts come from somewhere; they have a particular shape; and we perform certain tasks when we read them. We can explore questions related to each of those aspects: origin, text, reader. To ignore any of the three aspects is to cut ourselves off from valuable interpretive clues. This approach also fits our era. We live in a pluralistic world and society; and despite the resistance of those who in a sentimental and mistaken way yearn for some imaginary past, our world will become even more pluralistic. In such an era, methodological pluralism is entirely appropriate and evocative.

Some may view such pluralism with suspicion or even horror. I believe it is inevitable and helpful. I am not arguing, on the negative side, that meaning is indeterminate for texts, that we find ourselves in a chaotic state. I am arguing, on the positive side, that texts offer a richness of meaning, multiple meanings. That kind of diversity gives hope for the hermeneutical task in our pluralistic world.

A Hermeneutic of Curiosity. What I am proposing could then be called a hermeneutic of curiosity. Hermeneutics is like a detective investigating a mystery. In the search for interpretation, texts invite us to ask questions and explore. Texts say things that make us wonder. It is the text that becomes the window on its world of origin, on its own shape, and on readers in relation to it. So there is a textual base to this hermeneutic. As in the diagram above, the interpreter begins with the text which leads to questions of history (origin) and of structure and of relation to the reader. Each of the methods we use—whether textual, form, source, or canonical criticism with reference to origin or rhetorical criticism with reference to the text itself or reader-response criticism with reference to the reader—gives us a distinct angle of vision in the interpretive process. I have also said little about theological treatments of these texts. Biblical texts certainly make theological claims which invite that kind of analysis. Work with various methods generates various interpretations, or readings, of the text. Each reading is incomplete. It is not necessarily a failure, but it does not exhaust the text's possibilities. Thus all the different kinds of readings provide valuable information for the interpreter and so should receive attention.

This hermeneutic of curiosity requires that we give up the notion that there is one unitary meaning for a text and the optimism that we can determine that meaning. Texts generate multiple readings.[12] That kind of diversity provides greater opportunity for dialogue on the text and for appropriation of the text. Texts have various levels of meaning or layers to reveal. The call is to accept the pluralism of results in the interpretive task. Still, along with Ricoeur and Sternberg, I believe we can speak of a text's literary intent.[13] The text provides bases for evaluating our readings. Textual support is the criterion for judging our hermeneutical work. Perhaps this hermeneutic of curiosity can provide a way forward in our current debate.

Historical Perspective

The question I am proposing an answer to, then, is one of hermeneutics, the art of interpretation. The broader question of how to interpret texts is by no means new; it has a long history. In order to give some perspective to my proposal, let me rehearse the history of interpretation. This rehearsal will in no sense be exhaustive, but it will provide a backdrop; and I believe it will suggest that a hermeneutic of curiosity is consonant with the heritage of interpretation. The following survey will attend to the history of biblical literary scholarship, especially when related to (biblical) poetry. The title of this monograph promises treatment

---

[12]I agree with John Barton, "Classifying Biblical Criticism," *JSOT* 29 (1984): 19-35, who says that we are in an age in which interpreters produce "readings" of texts. In his volume *Reading the Old Testament*, Barton shows a greater concern for a historical referent for the text than would I. Meaning is generated in an interaction between text and reader. The plurality of meaning reflects various ways readers are called to live in continuity with the text.

[13]See Ricoeur, *Interpretation Theory*, 79, 92-95; Sternberg, *Poetics of Biblical Narrative*, 7-35, 41-57. David Clines's work on Isaiah 53 also speaks of the text creating a variety of meanings and yet still guiding the interpretive task and inviting the reader into a world the text creates: *I, He, We, & They: A Literary Approach to Isaiah 53*, JSOTSup 1 (Sheffield: JSOT Press, 1976) 59-60 and chap. 4.

of Psalm 61; it follows that our discussion should center on poetry and, where possible, psalmody. A look at the history of hermeneutics should facilitate our efforts to articulate an interpretive framework.

Precritical Era. The approach to the Bible used prior to the Enlightenment is typically characterized as "precritical"; a more accurate term would be "pre-Enlightenment." There was diversity in approach but probably enough commonality to justify dealing with these centuries together. The Bible was studied within the church, and interpreters spent much time on the language and sense of texts in the effort to apply them to their day. Historical aspects of the text were not ignored, but the primary search was for the deep spiritual meaning of passages from the Bible and their significance for that day. The text pointed beyond itself to the deeper reality of God. The purpose of the study of language and of history was to lead one to God. The assumption was that the words of the text stand for a reality beyond. History was noted but always with the purpose of encouraging love of God and/or neighbor. Text, language, and history led to meaning, a meaning beyond the text, a deeper spiritual reality.[14]

That kind of basis makes understandable the common use of allegory in those centuries. The text symbolized a deep spiritual meaning. Quoting Augustine, "Whatever in the text has nothing to do with right conduct or questions of faith must be understood figuratively."[15] Note his comment on the Genesis account of the flood:

> Under the sacramental sign of the flood, however, in which the righteous were rescued by the wood, there was also a fore-announcement of the Church which was to be, which Christ, its King and God, has raised on high, by the mystery of His cross, in safety from the submersion of this world.[16]

---

[14]See Edgar V. McKnight, *Postmodern Use of the Bible: The Emergence of Reader-Oriented Criticism* (Nashville: Abingdon Press, 1988) 29-44; Robert M. Grant with David Tracy, *A Short History of the Interpretation of the Bible*, 2nd ed. (Philadelphia: Fortress Press, 1984).

[15]*De Doctrina Christiana* 3.10.14., in vol. 2 of *A Select Library of the Nicene and Post-Nicene Fathers of the Christian Church*, ed. Philip Schaff (Grand Rapids MI: Eerdman's, 1956) 560.

[16]Augustine, *On the Catechising of the Uninstructed* 19.32, in vol. 3 of *Nicene and Post-Nicene Fathers*, 303; cited in McKnight, *Postmodern Use of the Bible*, 30.

Augustine's allegory represents much of pre-Enlightenment interpretation. The text supported and reflected the church's view of the world, a theocentric view. The referent of the text was a divine, spiritual reality, and the search for that reality provided the hermeneutical starting point.

The seeds of change in pre-critical interpretation were planted during the Reformation as a new humanism arose. Although the mode of interpretation was similar to that which had come before, the human condition as well as divine reality were to be discovered by investigation. Luther is illustrative. When he read the Psalter, it was not only the source of a theocentric reality, but also "a universal compendium of human emotion."[17]

> Fear and worry over what is to come, sorrow and sadness over present evil, hope and pride of future happiness, assurance and joy of things presently enjoyed–such are the winds that blow and teach the tongue to speak and open the heart to pour out its contents. In the Psalms the chief thing is such speaking in all manner of stormy winds. . . . Hence it comes about that in the booklet of all saints, and everybody in whatsoever situation he may be, finds Psalms and sayings in it that rhyme with his affairs, and seem to him as though they were formulated thus just for his sake.[18]

As can be readily seen, the Reformation brought about the winds of change, a change which not only affected the church, but biblical hermeneutics as well.

English Bishop Robert Lowth is a transitional figure connecting the precritical stage of biblical interpretation with its theocentric hermeneutic to the more critical awareness of the Enlightenment, especially in regards to biblical poetry.[19] While his intent was still theological, Lowth inte-

---

[17]James L. Kugel, *The Idea of Biblical Poetry: Parallelism and Its History* (New Haven/London: Yale University Press, 1981) 219.

[18]From the preface to Luther's translation of the Psalter (1531) as cited in E. G. Kraeling, *The Old Testament Since the Reformation* (New York: Harper & Row, 1955) 18.

[19]Robert Lowth's fundamental work *Prælectiones de sacra poësie Hebræorum* was published in 1753.

grated aesthetic standards into his treatment of the Bible.[20] Lowth is recognized as the biblical scholar who "rediscovered" the basic characteristics of parallelism in Hebrew poetry for modern scholarship.[21] He established the general guidelines—still widely used today—for a classification of parallelism into three broad categories: synonymous, antithetical, and synthetic.[22] Though influential, Lowth's categorization was of more importance on another front: it marked the beginning of critical analysis as to the *style* in which Hebrew poetry was written and the "discovery" of poetry beyond those books recognized as being poetical.[23] As Kugel states, "In this way, more than any other, Robert Lowth changed the way we read the Bible."[24]

Historical-Critical Era. The Reformation had begun to subvert the Roman Catholic Church's monolithic view of the world. With the rise of the Enlightenment, an emphasis on reason and on history brought a fundamental change in the view of the world dominant in western academic circles.[25] Interpreters came to believe that they could make trustworthy critical judgments. The task was not so much to proclaim the truth as to give the best, most probable, commentary on texts. Scholars also began to rediscover classical texts and works from antiquity. Historical context became the primary means for making critical judgments about cultures

---

[20]Kugel's discussion of Lowth's influence on subsequent interpretation of biblical poetry is beneficial. See Kugel, *Biblical Poetry*, 274-86.

[21]Peter C. Craigie, *Psalms 1-50*, WBC 19 (Waco TX: Word Books, 1983) 37. Lowth's work thus carries a historical-critical dimension.

[22]While the genius of Lowth's analysis may lie in its simplicity, it is not without its detractors. Note Kugel's comment: "This classification, far from illuminating, simply obscured the potential subtleties of the form: everything now fell into three boxes" (Kugel, *Biblical Poetry*, 12).

[23]Note the assessment of Lowth's contribution in George Buchanan Gray's *The Forms of Hebrew Poetry* (New York: KTAV, 1972) 6-7:

> Briefly summed up, Lowth's contribution to the subject was twofold: he for the first time clearly analyzed and expounded the parallelistic structure of Hebrew poetry, and he drew attention to the fact that the extent of poetry in the Old Testament was much larger than had generally been recognized.

[24]Kugel, *Biblical Poetry*, 286.

[25]See McKnight, *Postmodern Use of the Bible*, 44-53.

and literature. And what is more, those historical contexts came into being by way of a process. Just as contemporary persons experience historical processes, so did those in antiquity; and texts came out of those historical processes.

With the rise of the Enlightenment and its interest in history and reason, questions about external historical background had come to the fore in biblical studies. Since that time, dominant in Old Testament scholarship have been theories about the sources and backgrounds or settings from which texts derived. Can we trace the history of a text back to its origin and source? What was the intention of that text when it came to be? How was it put together and to what end? The search has been for the genesis, or origin, of the texts; and the assumption has been that when we find the original background of a passage, we have found the key to its interpretation. The historical critic insists that we begin the hermeneutical task by asking when and where and in what circumstances the text originated. Therein is the clue to its meaning.[26] The historical-critical approach has dominated biblical studies in the nineteenth and twentieth centuries.

Historical-critical work on the Psalms has been dominated by form-critical studies. The impetus for contemporary psalm study comes from the work of Hermann Gunkel.[27] Gunkel began by classifying the Psalms according to typical structures. That is his great contribution. We will consider the type/structure of Psalm 61. Gunkel also began to ask the question of where these types of psalms originated, the question of setting. Form-critical studies suggest that the key to discovering a text's intention is found in its background. That question was pursued by Gunkel's student Sigmund Mowinckel.[28] Mowinckel's view is that the Psalms arose and functioned within ancient Israel's cult. Their intention is firmly

---

[26]Krister Stendahl, "Biblical Theology, Contemporary," *IDB* (New York/Nashville: Abingdon Press, 1962) A-D:418-32, provides a classic statement of the historical-critical approach.

[27]See Hermann Gunkel, *The Psalms: A Form-Critical Introduction*, Facet Books, Biblical Series 19 (Philadelphia: Fortress Press, 1967); Claus Westermann, *Praise and Lament in the Psalms* (Atlanta: John Knox Press, 1981); R. E. Clements, *A Century of Old Testament Study* (London: Lutterworth, 1976) 76-98.

[28]See Sigmund Mowinckel, *The Psalms in Israel's Worship*, 2 vols., trans. D. R. Ap-Thomas (Nashville: Abingdon Press, 1962).

linked to that, primarily temple, worship. Questions of genre/structure and cultic function have thus dominated studies of the Psalms in the twentieth century, and we will consider their import for our study.

Along with the groundbreaking form-critical work of Gunkel and Mowinckel, a wide variety of approaches to Hebrew poetry were developing in critical circles, among them a concern especially for theories of meter.[29] Following the discovery of Ugaritic materials from Ras Shamra, a new era of the study of Hebrew poetry began as numerous scholars, beginning especially with W. F. Albright, incorporated insights from the study of Canaanite poetry into the study of ancient Israel's poetry.[30] Probably the foremost among these have been Frank Moore Cross[31] and Mitchell Dahood.[32] We will note more recent studies of Hebrew poetry in chapter 5.

Various standard surveys chronicle the rise of the historical-critical approach in biblical studies.[33] I have in this brief treatment sought to

---

[29]See the concise overview of three influential approaches in Otto Eissfeldt, *The Old Testament: An Introduction* (New York: Harper & Row, 1965) 60-63, to which now should be added the syllable-counting approach championed especially by Frank Moore Cross, Jr. and David Noel Freedman, described in their *Studies in Yahwistic Poetry*, SBLDS 21 (Missoula MT: Scholars Press, 1975) 185-86, and applied in many articles by each of them. For extensive bibliographies, see (for Freedman) *The Word of the Lord Shall Go Forth*, ed. Carol L. Meyers and Michael O'Connor (Philadelphia: ASOR, 1983) 721-25, and (for Cross) *Ancient Israelite Religion*, ed. Patrick D. Miller, Jr., Paul D. Hanson, and S. Dean McBride (Philadelphia: Fortress Press, 1987) 645-56.

[30]See, e.g., Albright's *Yahweh and the Gods of Canaan* (New York: Doubleday, 1969) 4-28.

[31]See esp. the articles collected in his *Canaanite Myth and Hebrew Epic* (Cambridge MA: Harvard University Press, 1973) 91-194.

[32]See esp. his provocative and frequently controversial commentary, *Psalms*, 3 vols., Anchor Bible (Garden City NY: Doubleday, 1966-1970).

[33]See Grant with Tracy, *A Short History of the Interpretation of the Bible*; Clements, *A Century of Old Testament Study*; Klaus Koch, *The Book of Books: The Growth of the Biblical Tradition*, trans. Margaret Kohl (Philadelphia: Westminster Press, 1968); Robert Davidson and A. R. C. Leaney, *Biblical Criticism*, Pelican Guide to Modern Theology 3 (Hammondsworth: Penguin, 1970). Several volumes in the Guides to Biblical Scholarship series (GBS) from Fortress Press also provide helpful background. John Barton, *Reading the Old Testament*, 1-76,

describe the approach in relation to that which came before, to indicate its base in a view of the world spawned by the Enlightenment, and to highlight the centrality of historical judgments in its view of the interpretive task. The dominance of the historical-critical approach is, however, beginning to show some notable cracks.

This development is also notable in psalm studies. To limit the task of psalm interpretation to historical-critical concerns is to lock the interpreter in a past constructed from our vantage point. Some recent studies have begun to move beyond questions of origin.[34] Canonical analyses have begun to ask the question of what happened to the psalm after its origin. How did it get to its place in the canonical book of Psalms? What is the significance of its canonical context?[35] Perhaps the most prominent scholar asking questions such as these is Brevard Childs. Childs has linked the process of interpretation with the Bible's canonical context and with the ways in which the community shaped these texts into the canonical books.[36] Other recent studies, following the lead of Bishop Lowth in the area of aesthetics, have considered the poetic nature of the psalms in rhetorical or formal analyses, concentrating on the text itself. This movement has a tradition of its own.

The New Criticism. Challenges to the dominance of the historical-critical approach have come from a variety of directions. Of particular

---

provides constructive comment on the purposes of historical-critical tools.

[34]See W. H. Bellinger, Jr., *Psalms: Reading and Studying the Book of Praises* (Peabody MA: Hendrickson Publishers, 1990) 27-43, for an account of these recent movements.

[35]The Society of Biblical Literature Book of Psalms Group has begun in the last five years to explore these issues in productive ways. Three works on the Psalms are of particular note here: J. Clinton McCann, ed., *The Shape and Shaping of the Psalter*, JSOTSup 159 (Sheffield: Sheffield Academic Press, 1993); McCann, *A Theological Introduction to the Book of Psalms: The Psalms as Torah* (Nashville: Abingdon Press, 1993); and the entire April 1992 issue of the journal *Interpretation* (46/2) on "The Book of Psalms."

[36]See especially B. S. Childs, *Biblical Theology in Crisis* (Philadelphia: Westminster Press, 1970); *Introduction to the Old Testament as Scripture* (Philadelphia: Fortress Press, 1979); and "The Exegetical Significance of Canon for the Study of the Old Testament," *Congress Volume, Göttingen 1977*, VTSup 29 (Leiden: E. J. Brill, 1978) 66-80.

importance is a development in the discipline of literary criticism in this century, an Anglo-American movement called the New Criticism.[37] Its advocates reacted against a biographical or historically-oriented interpretation of texts. In a famous essay entitled "The Intentional Fallacy," W. K. Wimsatt and M. C. Beardsley argued that external influences in the life of an author, events contemporaneous with the writing of a document, should not be used as the interpretive key when seeking to understand a text.[38] Indeed, to seek to uncover an author's intent in light of external considerations is not possible; it would require us to read the mind of the author. The New Critics thus moved away from questions of authorial intent and historical background in interpreting texts.

In place of concern with questions of origin and historical backgrounds of texts, the New Critics concentrated on the shape of the text itself. A text has an independent life as a system of values.[39] A text is an autonomous whole, not dependent on historical settings. Interpreters study the text itself without external reference. The emphasis is on the structural unity of the text. This movement has its base in such signifi-

---

[37]See Rene Welleck and Austin Warren, *Theory of Literature*, A Harvest Book (New York: Harcourt, Brace, and Co., 1942); W. K. Wimsatt, Jr., *The Verbal Icon: Studies in the Meaning of Poetry* (London: Methuen & Co., 1970 [University of Kentucky Press, 1954]); David Newton-de Molina, ed., *On Literary Intention* (Edinburgh: Edinburgh University Press, 1976); E. M. W. Tillyard and C. S. Lewis, *The Personal Heresy: A Controversy* (London/New York/Toronto: Oxford University Press, 1939); C. S. Lewis, *An Experiment in Criticism* (Cambridge: Cambridge University Press, 1961).

[38]First published in 1946 and reprinted in *On Literary Intention*.

[39]Wellek and Warren, *Theory of Literature*, 31. Note also the epigraph in Barton, *Reading the Old Testament*, 140:

We have entered a universe that answers to its own laws, supports itself, internally coheres, and has a new standard of truth. Information is true if it is accurate. A poem is true if it hangs together. Information points to something else. A poem points to nothing but itself. Information is relative. A poem is absolute.

—E. M. Forster, *Anonymity: an Inquiry* (London 1925) 14.

cant literary figures as T. S. Eliot,[40] but it has had significant influence in biblical studies.

In such a "text-immanent" approach, the task is to see the unity of the text in its various parts. The search is for movement, plot, and stylistic devices in the text. What strategies does the text use in communicating its message? The tone of a text and shifts therein, paradox, irony, humor, and other aspects of the text are significant in the New Critics' reading of a text. How does such an investigation help us to see the text as a whole? The view of the New Criticism strikes a contrast to that of the historical-critical approach. The questions are not of origin. Meaning is now inherent in the language and structures of the text.[41]

The New Criticism is no longer a priority in literary criticism, but it has left a significant mark in biblical studies. A number of recent works point to the literary features of the poetry in the Psalter: parallelism, repetition, word play, ambiguity, figures of speech. Chief among these is the

---

[40]See T. S. Eliot, *On Poetry and Poets* (London: Faber and Faber, 1957). Barton, *Reading the Old Testament*, 148, notes the following anecdote in Stephen Spender, "Remembering Eliot," *T. S. Eliot: The Man and His Work*, ed. Allen Tate, A Seymour Lawrence Book (New York: Delacorte Press, 1966) 42:

Even Eliot could be less than helpful if one tried to "explicate" him. In 1929, there was a meeting of the Oxford Poetry Club at which he was the guest of honour. Before it, some of us arranged a separate meeting with Father M. C. D'Arcy, with whom we studied the text of *Ash-Wednesday*, just published. Some points were not cleared up, and at the later meeting an undergraduate asked Eliot: "Please, sir, what do you mean by the line: *Lady, three white leopards sat under a juniper tree?*" Eliot looked at him and said: "I mean, *Lady, three white leopards sat under a juniper tree.*"

[41]See McKnight, *Postmodern Use of the Bible*, 131-34; Barton, *Reading the Old Testament*, 140-97. Barton notes difficulties with the New Criticism. Some work has also been done in this area in German: M. Weiss, "Wege der neuen Dichtungswissenschaft in ihrer Auswendung auf die Psalmen Forschung," *Biblica* 42 (1961): 255-302; idem, "Die Methode der 'Total-Interpretation'," *Congress Volume, Uppsala 1971*, VTSup 22 (Leiden: E. J. Brill, 1972) 88-112; Wolfgang Richter, *Exegese als Literaturwissenschaft: Entwurf einer alttestamentlichen Literatur Theorie und Methodologie* (Göttingen: Vandenhoeck & Ruprecht, 1971).

work of Robert Alter.[42] Such studies partake of a tradition that reaches back to Lowth. Still one of the profound effects of the New Criticism is that it has raised many questions about historical-critical studies and has brought to the fore a text-immanent approach.

Structuralism. Overlapping with the development of the New Criticism, the movement called structuralism began to exert influence in European literary and philosophical circles.[43] Structuralists also moved away from concern with authors and historical background. These interpreters argued that texts are expressions of a system of human communication. Thus structuralist interpretations reflect on how a text uses the system of language to communicate its message. Rolande Barthes, a leading structuralist, has even described structuralism as the death of the author.[44]

Structuralists have not concentrated on poetry, perhaps because poems tend to be distinctive works, and structuralists tend to see works in a coherent, more impersonal way. Such interpreters do, however, note the devices in poems, their poetic structures, and thematic significance. It is the use of the structures of the language system that enables the

---

[42]See Alter, *The Art of Biblical Poetry* (New York: Basic Books, 1985); Alter, "Psalms," *The Literary Guide to the Bible,* ed. Robert Alter and Frank Kermode (Cambridge MA: Harvard University Press, 1987) 251-55. Also of interest, though pertaining to the literary artistry of Hebrew poetry in the prophetic corpus, are two works in the series Literary Currents in Biblical Interpretation by Katheryn Pfister Darr, *Isaiah's Vision and the Family of God* (Louisville: Westminster/John Knox Press, 1994) and Thomas Jemielity, *Satire and the Hebrew Prophets* (Louisville: Westminster/John Knox Press, 1992).

[43]I have not mentioned formalism; but as the surveys of literary criticism indicate, the work of the various formalists has significant connections with both the New Criticism and structuralism and serves as a significant part of the background to contemporary literary theory. Semiotics is also part of the picture.

[44]Rolande Barthes, "The Death of the Author," *Image—Music—Text,* ed. and trans. Stephen Heath (New York: Hill & Wang, 1977) 142-48. See also Ferdinand de Saussure, *Course in General Linguistics,* ed. Charles Bally and Albert Secheharge in collaboration with Albert Reidlinger, trans. Wade Baskin (New York: Philosophical Library, 1959); Robert Detweiler, *Story, Sign, and Self: Phenomenology and Structuralism as Literary-Critical Methods* (Missoula MT: Scholars Press, 1978).

reader to imaginatively interpret poetic texts.[45] John Barton is right when he insists that structuralism is properly a theory about reading texts.[46] Readers use the conventions, structures, of the language system to make sense of texts. Thus the referent of texts is found in the system of linguistic conventions agreed upon by readers. Structuralism is a complicated theory and has received various explanations, but this brief description should demonstrate its challenge to the historical-critical approach. The emphasis on linguistic or structural conventions and on the process of reading move the task of interpretation away from questions of origin and historical background.

Both the New Criticism and structuralism have appropriately faded from the scene, but they have left their mark on literary studies in general and biblical studies in particular.[47] They have especially challenged the dominance of the historical-critical approach. In the wake of their demise, we have seen the rise of a variety of approaches in reading texts.

Post-structuralism. The hermeneutical developments I have been tracing have raised serious questions about the dominant historical-critical approach, but neither structuralism nor the New Criticism has succeeded in garnering a consensus for a new approach. Their influence is waning, but few hermeneutical theorists would return to a historical approach. A variety of approaches is now in view, with no one holding sway.

Probably the approach that is the heir to structuralism is that of deconstruction, most often associated with Jacques Derrida.[48] A text re-

---

[45]See Jonathan Culler, *Structuralist Poetics: Structuralism, Linguistics and the Study of Literature* (London: Routledge & Kegan Paul, 1975) esp. 161-88. McKnight, *The Bible and the Reader*, 56-58, has noted that Barthes emphasizes the particularity of texts; Barthes eventually moved beyond structuralism. See also Terence Collins, "Decoding the Psalms: A Structural Approach to the Psalter," *JSOT* 37 (1987): 41-60.

[46]Barton, *Reading the Old Testament*, 104-39.

[47]See McKnight, *Postmodern Use of the Bible*, 115-31; R. M. Polzin, *Biblical Structuralism: Method and Subjectivity in the Study of Ancient Texts* (Philadelphia: Fortress Press, 1977); Christopher Norris, *Deconstruction: Theory and Practice* (New Accents; New York/London: Methuen & Co., 1982) 15.

[48]See Jacques Derrida, "Différance," *Margins of Philosophy*, trans. Alan Bass (Chicago: University of Chicago Press, 1982) and *Of Grammatology*, trans. Gayatri C. Spivak (Baltimore/London: Johns Hopkins University Press, 1974) and

flects a system of language, but that system is part of a larger set of conventions which can be evaluated. Thus any construction of a text's meaning can be questioned. There is no real foundation for knowledge. Meanings of texts are indeterminate; our knowledge is limited. This deconstructive approach has been applied to biblical texts.[49] Scholars have pealed back layers of texts to find basic assertions which do not mesh. Disorder thus replaces the order of the earlier structuralism. Earlier readings of texts are questioned. Culler suggests that deconstruction raises significant theoretical issues about the categories used to interpret texts and encourages readers to see conflicts within texts.[50] Deconstruction has raised significant questions for interpreters, but it does not offer a significant way forward in the attempt to articulate the relation between text and reader.

A more constructive way forward is that of reader response criticism. The significance of the reader in the process of interpretation has begun to come to the fore.[51] Readers bring concerns with them to the reading

---

The Post Card: From Socrates to Freud and Beyond, trans. Alan Bass (Chicago: University of Chicago Press, 1987); Jonathan Culler, *On Deconstruction: Theory and Criticism After Structuralism* (London: Routledge & Kegan Paul, 1983); Art Berman, *From the New Criticism to Deconstruction: The Reception of Structuralism and Post-Structuralism* (Chicago: University of Illinois Press, 1988); William Ray, *Literary Meaning: From Phenomenology to Deconstruction* (Oxford: Basil Blackwell, 1984); McKnight, *The Bible and the Reader,* 84-94.

[49]See Peter D. Miscall, *1 Samuel: A Literary Reading,* Indiana Studies in Biblical Literature (Bloomington: Indiana University Press, 1986); Danna Nolan Fewell, "Feminist Reading of the Hebrew Bible: Affirmation, Resistance, and Transformation," *JSOT* 39 (1987): 77-87; idem, *Circle of Sovereignty: Plotting Politics in the Book of Daniel* (Nashville: Abingdon Press, 1991).

[50]Jonathan Culler, *Framing the Sign: Criticism and Its Institutions,* Oklahoma Project for Discourse and Theory (Norman OK/London: University of Oklahoma Press, 1988) 20.

[51]See Umberto Eco, *The Role of the Reader: Explorations in the Semiotics of Texts* (Bloomington, IN: Indiana University Press, 1979); Jane P. Tompkins, ed., *Reader-Response Criticism: From Formalism to Post-Structuralism* (Baltimore: Johns Hopkins University Press, 1980); Susan R. Suleiman and Inge Crosman, eds., *The Reader in the Text: Essays on Audience and Interpretation* (Princeton: Princeton University Press, 1980); Steven Mailloux, *Interpretive Conventions: The Reader in the Study of American Fiction* (Ithaca NY/London: Cor-

of texts and those concerns from the context of the reader exert significant influence in interpretation. One's interpretive community, whether it be feminist, Marxist, or evangelical, exercises power in the interpretive act.[52] Other theorists have taken a more phenomenological approach to the process of reading.[53] What patterns do interpreters use in the act of reading? Edgar McKnight has chronicled the emergence of the importance of the reader and the significance of this movement for biblical studies.[54]

Psychoanalysis has become important in contemporary literary theory.[55] Speech-act theory and a New Historicism and other methodologies have also entered the fray. Contemporary criticism is keenly aware of its political dimensions.[56]

Post-structuralist interpretation has many faces, but probably the common aspect to all post-structuralist approaches to hermeneutics is that

---

nell University Press, 1982); Robert Detweiler, ed., *Reader Response Approaches to Biblical and Secular Texts, Semeia* 31 (Atlanta: Scholars Press, 1985).

[52]See Stanley Fish, *Is There a Text in This Class? The Authority of Interpretive Communities* (Cambridge MA: Harvard University Press, 1982). For illustrative psalms representing an understanding of the use of social and political power within these texts, see J. David Pleins, *The Psalms: Songs of Tragedy, Hope, and Justice* (Maryknoll NY: Orbis Books, 1994). Also of interest is Ernesto Cardenal, *Psalms* (New York: Crossroad, 1981).

[53]Wolfgang Iser, *The Implied Reader: Patterns of Communication in Prose Fiction from Bunyan to Beckett* (Baltimore: Johns Hopkins University Press, 1974); idem, *The Act of Reading: A Theory of Aesthetic Response* (Baltimore: Johns Hopkins Univesity Press, 1978); idem, "Indeterminacy and the Reader's Response in Prose Fiction," *Aspects of Narrative*, ed. J. Hillis Miller, English Institute Essays (New York: Columbia University Press, 1971) 1-45. See also Barbara Herrnstein Smith, *Poetic Closure: A Study of How Poems End* (Chicago: University of Chicago Press, 1968).

[54]See McKnight, *The Bible and the Reader* and *Postmodern Use of the Bible*.

[55]See, e.g., Norman N. Holland, *Poems in Persons: An Introduction to the Psychoanalysis of Literature* (New York: W. W. Norton & Co., 1973) and *5 Readers Reading* (New Haven: Yale University Press, 1975).

[56]Two surveys of literary theory are especially helpful at this point: Culler, *Framing the Sign*, 3-40, and Terry Eagleton, *Literary Theory: An Introduction* (Minneapolis: University of Minnesota Press, 1983).

interpreters "create" meaning in the reading process.[57] That is a far cry from the dominance of the historical-critical approach.

Conclusion. Common to the work of the New Critics, structuralists, and those who could be seen as part of the various post-structuralist currents is a move away from an obsession with the "original intent" of a text as determined by an external historical setting. Rather, after they are put into writing, texts take on a life of their own; they are not simply tied to one original setting and intent but generate various meanings or readings. The word is "multivalence"; texts express multiple meanings.

An exception to that would be the work of E. D. Hirsch, who has written in defense of the author whose intent provides, in Hirsch's view, the determinative meaning of a text.[58] Authorial intent determines meaning, though the significance or application of a text may change from time to time. An interpretation is valid when it coheres and is appropriate to the text's genre and corresponds with the author's intent. Hirsch has made a significant contribution to the conversation, but too many questions have been raised about an original authorial intent to justify retreating to such a historically dominated view.

Frank Lentricchia has surveyed the history of literary criticism between 1957 and 1977—traditional, New Critical, structuralist, and post-structuralist interpretation.[59] His conclusion is that contemporary interpre-

---

[57]Harold Fisch's *Poetry with a Purpose: Biblical Poetics and Interpretation* (Bloomington/Indianapolis: University of Indiana Press, 1988) offers a creative example of poststructuralist exegetical work. See esp. his chapter on the Psalms, 104-35. Walter Brueggemann's two works, *Israel's Praise: Doxology against Idolatry and Ideology* (Philadelphia: Fortress Press, 1988) and *Abiding Astonishment: Psalms, Modernity, and the Making of History*, Literary Currents in Biblical Interpretation (Louisville: Westminster/John Knox Press, 1991) also reflect post-structuralist leanings.

[58]E. D. Hirsch, Jr., *Validity in Interpretation* (New Haven: Yale University Press, 1967) and *The Aims of Interpretation* (Chicago: University of Chicago Press, 1976). Northrop Frye has also sought to bring some order to the results of interpretation with his emphasis on archetypes or myths. See his *Anatomy of Criticism* (Princeton: Princeton University Press, 1957) and *The Great Code: The Bible and Literature* (London: Routledge & Kegan Paul, 1982).

[59]Frank Lentricchia, *After the New Criticism* (Chicago: University of Chicago Press, 1980).

ters must come to terms with the multiplicity of readings which texts generate. That view is a more realistic one.

When we apply the perspective of these recent developments in literary criticism, I am now convinced that the time in which we found the key for interpretation in a text's original historical setting and authorial intent is past. The absolute reign of the historical-critical approach is over. What the author meant can no longer provide the clue for meaning. That conclusion has important implications for biblical studies. In a 1976 study, David Clines noted that poetic texts often did not provide what historical critics sought anyway.[60] A poetic text, in this case Isaiah 53, contains ambiguities and enigmas. Its purpose is not to answer the questions of historical critics. Clines argues that interpreters should focus on the text and its use of language rather than on questions of original context. The text has a life of its own and so creates a variety of meanings in relation to readers. Clines's work is reminiscent of that of Paul Ricoeur.[61] Ricoeur agrees that texts take on a life of their own and enable multiple readings. The referent for meaning is not the historical background of the text but the "world" which the text creates as a way for readers to view life. The multiple readings speak to various dimensions of that world.

The works of Clines and Ricoeur focus attention on the primary question in the hermeneutical debate raging today. What is the locus of meaning? Certainly authors intended meaning when they wrote, but attempts to discover those intents are essentially marred. When a text becomes written, it does take on a life of its own because it is read in many ways. Affirmation of the multiplicity of meanings for texts from the original meaning of the writer to that of the latest reader seems inescapable. It is a part of the literary quality of texts. The search for meaning

---

[60]Clines, *I, He, We, & They*, 25, and the whole volume.

[61]Paul Ricoeur, *Interpretation Theory* and *The Rule of Metaphor: Multidisciplinary Studies of the Creation of Meaning in Language*, trans. Robert Czerny with Kathleen McLaughlin and John Costello (London: Routledge & Kegan Paul, 1978); *Essays on Biblical Interpretation*, ed. with an introduction by Lewis S. Mudge (London: SPCK, 1981); *The Conflict of Interpretations: Essays in Hermeneutics*, ed. Don Ihde (Evanston: Northwestern University Press, 1974); John Dominic Crossan, ed., *Paul Ricoeur and Biblical Hermeneutics, Semeia* 4 (Missoula MT: Scholars Press, 1975).

solely in questions of origin is unsatisfying. If, however, we leave the model of the historical-critical approach, where are we to go? Are we simply left adrift at sea with no charts for interpretation? How shall we interpret or read texts, in this case, biblical texts?[62] It is in response to this dilemma that I offer the constructive proposal of a hermeneutic of curiosity.

A hermeneutic of curiosity will lead the interpreter to ask many different questions of the text, questions stemming from the rich heritage of interpretation. This course of action necessitates a methodological pluralism that will investigate the three-fold aspect of origin, text, and reader. To ignore any of these three dimensions and their hermeneutical traditions is to fail in attempting a wholistic interpretive approach. The results of applying a hermeneutic of curiosity will be a medley of readings and a fuller dialogue with the text. Further, the individual reader will have a greater appreciation for the task of interpretation and an understanding of how it is impossible to exhaust the possibilities presented by the text.

The Plan of the Book

From the hermeneutical framework described in this introduction, we will move to an extended treatment of Psalm 61. Questions of origin will dominate the next chapters. A translation and discussion of text-critical issues are in the appendix and provide a basis for the study. In chapters 2 and 3 will come the concerns of form criticism: type/structure first and then setting. We will then consider a canonical analysis in chapter 4, which will provide the transition to a look in chapter 5 at more "text-immanent" approaches to the psalm. Chapter 6 will then consider reader-oriented approaches to the psalm. Chapter 7 will examine the text from theological perspectives. We will then conclude with broader hermeneutical reflections on the project.

The agenda of this volume, then, includes several issues. I am especially concerned with hermeneutical issues. Are there ways to move

---

[62]See Regina M. Schwartz, "Introduction: On Biblical Criticism," *The Book and the Text: The Bible and Literary Theory* (Oxford: Basil Blackwell, 1990) for discussion of the current status and context of interpretation. R. Alan Culpepper, "Commentary on Biblical Narratives: Changing Paradigms," *Forum* 5 (1989): 87-102, has also chronicled recent shifts in biblical interpretation.

forward in the current debate? We will consider such questions in our treatment of Psalm 61. I am also concerned with questions of method in the analysis of poetic texts in the Hebrew Bible. More recent literary approaches have found the analysis of poetic texts less fruitful than that of narrative texts. What progress can we make in the analysis of poetry? We will also press forward to the question of the reader in the Psalms. Little has been done on reader-response criticism in the Psalms.

I am also concerned about Psalm 61. Why do I choose this psalm? Hermeneutical theories and interpretive methodologies meet their real test in the treatment of texts; otherwise they are but obscure musings. In a sense, this volume is an experiment, a test case. Will my hermeneutic of curiosity lead to fruitful analysis and reflection on Psalm 61? If so, perhaps the framework will bear wider significance. But why this particular psalm? It is, in many ways, a typical psalm. It has much in common with other laments and relates to a variety of significant issues in psalm study. I have long had an interest in psalms of innocence, and Psalm 61 fits that category. Questions of temple and land and kingship are also important. The psalm is thus a representative text for theory and method.

For years Psalm 61 has intrigued me. It will provide a limited test for this experiment. In many ways this study will be a test of methods in the context of the hermeneutic of curiosity described in this introduction.[63] I hope the study will contribute to contemporary discussions in biblical studies.

---

[63]For a concise description of the various methods, see Walter Beyerlin, *Weisheitlich-kultische Heilsordnung: Studien zum 15. Psalm*, Biblisch-Theologische Studien 9 (Neukirchen-Vluyn: Neukirchener Verlag, 1985).

Form

Introduction

Our first approaches in interpreting Psalm 61 will remain within the confines of the form-critical task as traditionally established in psalm scholarship. That task begins with determining the unit under consideration, then considers the structure through which the text moves, and comes to a decision as to the genre (or *Gattung*) of the psalm. This chapter will consider these matters. Chapter 3 ("Setting") will treat the *Sitz im Leben*.

The text invites us to consider these issues. When we read the book of which Psalm 61 is a part, we meet both confusing variety and conventional monotony. How does Psalm 61 relate to the other psalms?[1] Where does one begin in interpreting such a text and on what basis? What does a reader expect when reading the psalm?[2] What is the movement of the psalm and how do its various parts relate? These questions are basic to the task of interpretation, and a form-critical approach can help us begin to answer them.

---

[1]The form-critical classification of the Psalms helps organize a study of the whole Psalter by grouping together psalms of the same *Gattung*. Such classification enables one to study a particular psalm in light of other similar poems. See Gunkel, *The Psalms*; Hermann Gunkel and Joachim Begrich, *Einleitung in die Psalmen* (Göttingen: Vandenhoeck & Ruprecht, 1933); D. J. A. Clines, "Psalm Research Since 1955: II. The Literary Genres," *TynBul* 20 (1969): 105-25; Bellinger, *Psalms*, 15-26.

[2]See John Barton, *Reading the Old Testament*, 30-44, for a helpful treatment of the purposes and limitations of form criticism. Barton and Gene M. Tucker, *Form Criticism of the Old Testament*, GBS (Philadelphia: Fortress Press, 1971) emphasize reader expectation.

The Unit

First we should determine the unit under consideration. Psalm 61 is a discrete text. Note the formal markers. No textual tradition considers the psalm as a part of any other text. The manuscripts treat Psalm 61 as a separate unit. In addition, note that the text begins with a superscription as do most of the psalms in the first two books of the Psalter. Psalm 60, before our text, and Psalm 62, after it, are also set off with superscriptions. The external markers indicate that Psalm 61 is a unit.

Also note the internal markers. Verse 2 of the psalm is an address to God and an introductory cry for help. Many of the psalms begin in just such a manner, further indication of a clear unit. The final verse of the psalm also indicates closure of a text with the concluding use of כֵּן and with the reference to vows. Many typical psalmic prayers conclude with vows of praise. In addition, compare the beginning of the psalm with its conclusion. The speaker begins by seeking God's ear and concludes by also seeking the divine ear. The psalm begins, however, with a cry for help and concludes with a song of praise, both addressed to God. The psalm begins by seeking God's help and concludes with fulfilling vows to God, future acts of faith. The "plot" of the text is complete. The issue has come to a clear resolution. So the internal markings of Psalm 61 also indicate that it is a discrete text for form-critical analysis.

The Structure

Consider the following typical comment on the structure of Psalm 61:

> It begins with a call for help (verses 1-2 [H 2-3]), and gives a passing glimpse at the distress of the Psalmist. Verses 3-4 [H 4-5] utter a firm trust in God and a fervent wish for a better future. This is followed by an expression of confidence that God has heard the prayer (verse 5 [H 6]); or it could be taken as a continuation of the supplication. In verses 6-7 [H 7-8] we find a brief prayer on behalf of the King, and the Psalm concludes on a note of trust and certitude (verse 8 [H 9]).[3]

H.-J. Kraus describes a similar structure:

---

[3]A. A. Anderson, *The Book of Psalms*, vol. 1, NCB (London: Oliphants, 1972) 446-47.

	Title
vv. 1-2 [H 2-3]	Address
vv. 3-4 [H 4-5]	Trust and wish
vv. 5, 8 [H 6, 9]	Certainty to be heard
vv. 6-7 [H 7-8]	Intercession for the king[4]

A survey of the commentaries, however, reveals no unanimity on the structure of the psalm. Note the following possibilities for the subunits. (The Hebrew versification is used here, even though the commentator may have used English versification.)

Gunkel	vv. 2-3 / 4-5 / 6, 9[5]
Deissler	vv. 2-3 / 4-5 / 6-9[6]
Eaton	vv. 2-3 / 4-6 / 7-9[7]
Weiser	vv. 2-3 / 4-5 / 6 / 7-8 / 9[8]
Schmidt	vv. 2-4 / 5-6, 9[9]
Taylor, et. al.	vv. 2-4 / 5-6 / 9[10]
Dahood	vv. 2-4 / 5-9[11]
Oesterley	vv. 2-4 / 5-6 / 7-8 / 9[12]
Delitzsch	vv. 2-5 / 6-9[13]

---

[4]Hans-Joachim Kraus, *Psalms 60–150: A Commentary*, trans. Hilton C. Oswald (Minneapolis: Augsburg/Fortress Press, 1989) 8.

[5]Hermann Gunkel, *Die Psalmen*, GHK 2 (Göttingen: Vandenhoeck & Ruprecht, 1926) 260-61. He considers vv. 7-8 as a later addition to the psalm.

[6]Alfons Deissler, *Die Psalmen*, Die Welt der Bibel (Düsseldorf: Patsmos-Verlag, 1963) 237.

[7]J. H. Eaton, *Psalms*, TBC (London: SCM Press, 1967) 157.

[8]Artur Weiser, *The Psalms: A Commentary*, OTL (London: SCM Press; Philadelphia: Westminster Press, 1959) 443-45.

[9]Hans Schmidt, *Die Psalmen*, HAT (Tübingen: J. C. B. Mohr [Paul Siebeck], 1934) 116. Schmidt treats vv. 7-8 separately.

[10]William R. Taylor and W. Stewart McCullough, "The Book of Psalms," *IB* (New York/Nashville: Abingdon Press, 1955) 4:318. Verses 7-8 are an addition.

[11]Dahood, *Psalms*, 2:84.

[12]W. O. E. Oesterley, *The Psalms* (London: SPCK, 1953) 300-301.

[13]Franz Delititzsch, *Biblical Commentary on the Psalms*, trans. David Eaton (London: Hodder & Stoughton, 1902) 229-30.

Kirkpatrick   vv. 2-5 / 6-9[14]

This list is but a sampling of the commentaries, but a wide variety is already noticeable. What the interpreter does with the prayer for the king (vv. 7-8) and how it relates to the concluding verse has a significant impact on interpretation. The situation is complicated by the view of various commentators that the prayer in vv. 7-8 is a later addition. For the moment, let us consider the psalm as a whole since we have established that it is a discrete unit. There is no textual tradition with parts of the psalm omitted. The question of redaction will arise again later. Important connections with the translation of the Hebrew also come into play (see the appendix, below). How the interpreter construes pivotal words and especially how one understands the syntax of verbs in the psalm have a great impact on one's view of the psalm's structure. One noticeable example is how one relates v. 4 and v. 6, both of which begin with כִּי, to the verses before and after them. כִּי could give motivation for the petition which precedes or which follows. A number of interpreters take the כִּי that begins v. 6 as the turning point in the movement of the psalm. From this point on, confidence in answered prayer dominates. But this reading is not the only possibility.[15]

One way forward in the attempt to discern the structure of the psalm is, in addition to the traditional form-critical categories, to factor in the poetic devices in the text. These stylistic or rhetorical devices may provide clues to structure. That is to say, our consideration of the structure of Psalm 61 ought to include not only the text's typical, or generic, patterns but also its distinctive poetic style. A number of contemporary practitioners of form criticism suggest that such stylistic devices provide hearers/readers with structural markers in the text.[16] This perspective

---

[14]A. F. Kirkpatrick, ed., *The Book of Psalms*, CBSC (Cambridge: Cambridge University Press, 1902) 344.

[15]Anderson, *Psalms*, 1:447, notes two possible readings of v. 6.

[16]See Paul Mosca, "Psalm 26: Poetic Structure and the Form-Critical Task," *CBQ* 47 (1985): 212-37; W. H. Bellinger, Jr., "Psalm 26: A Test of Method," *VT* 43 (1993): 452-61; G. S. Ogden, "Psalm 60: Its Rhetoric, Form, and Function," *JSOT* 31 (1985): 83-94; Craig C. Broyles, *The Conflict of Faith and Experience in the Psalms: A Form-Critical and Theological Study*, JSOTSup 52 (Sheffield: Sheffield Academic Press, 1989); R. F. Melugin, "Muilenburg, Form Criticism,

dates back to the suggestions of Muilenburg,[17] and we will pursue it in our discussion of structure. Consider the following proposal for the structure of Psalm 61.

לַמְנַצֵּחַ עַל־נְגִינַת לְדָוִד:

1. To the Choirmaster. Upon stringed instruments. Of David.

Verse 1 is the superscription to the psalm and so is outside the poetic structure. Upon this point there is unanimity. Many psalms have such titles written above the text.

A helpful way to discern structure is to look for poetic markers that indicate significant turns in the movement of the text. The psalm begins with שְׁמְעָה אֱלֹהִים "Hear, O God." The response to the prayer is in v. 6, כִּי־אַתָּה אֱלֹהִים שָׁמַעְתָּ "Indeed, you, O God, have heard." So v. 6 marks a major structural break.[18] There is a further division in vv. 2-6 in that v. 4 provides, beginning with כִּי, the motivation for the preceding prayer.[19] So vv. 2-4 and vv. 5-6 make up the first two "verse paragraphs" in Psalm 61.[20] The third section, vv. 7-9, is marked off with the inclusio

---

and Theological Exegesis," in *Encounter with the Text: Form and History in the Hebrew Bible*, ed. M. J. Buss, *Semeia* (Philadelphia: Fortress; Missoula MT: Scholars Press, 1979) 91-102; David Greenwood, "Rhetorical Criticism and *Formsgeschichte*: Some Methodological Considerations," *JBL* 89 (1970): 418-26.

[17]J. Muilenburg, "Form Criticism and Beyond," *JBL* 88 (1969): 1-18; "A Study in Hebrew Rhetoric: Repetition and Style," *Congress Volume*, VTSup 1 (Leiden: E. J. Brill, 1953) 97-111; and "The Linguistic and Rhetorical Usages of the Particle כִּי in the Old Testament," *HUCA* 32 (1963): 135. Muilenburg's program concentrated on determining the unit and structure of a text. Form criticism continues to the genre, setting, and intent.

[18]Such an *inclusio* often marks closure in a psalm. See Muilenburg, "Hebrew Rhetoric," 99; idem, "Form Criticism and Beyond," 9; Mosca, "Psalm 26," 220-22; Alter, "Psalms," 255-56.

[19]See Muilenburg, "Particle כִּי," 154.

[20]I use the term "verse paragraph" in the same way as Mosca, "Psalm 26," 223 n. 37: "a group of lines, frequently in blank verse, arranged as a rhetorical unit similar to a paragraph in prose." Mosca's definition comes from K. Beckson and A. Ganz, *A Reader's Guide to Literary Terms: A Dictionary* (New York: Farrar, Straus, & Giroux, 1960) 226. The major break is at the end of v. 6, but there is sufficient shift after v. 4 to justify treating vv. 2-4 and vv. 5-6 separately.

יָמִים עַל־יְמֵי: "Days upon days" (v. 7) and יוֹם יוֹם "day by day" (v. 9).[21]

I.

² שִׁמְעָה אֱלֹהִים רִנָּתִי
הַקְשִׁיבָה תְּפִלָּתִי:
³ מִקְצֵה הָאָרֶץ אֵלֶיךָ אֶקְרָא בַּעֲטֹף לִבִּי
בְּצוּר־יָרוּם מִמֶּנִּי תַנְחֵנִי:
⁴ כִּי־הָיִיתָ מַחְסֶה לִי
מִגְדַּל־עֹז מִפְּנֵי אוֹיֵב:

²Hear, O God, my cry;
   attend to my prayer.
³From the end of the earth I call unto you when my heart is faint;
   lead me to a rock high beyond me,
⁴for you have been a refuge for me,
   a strong tower in the face of the enemy.

The first section of the psalm, vv. 2-4, opens with a plea.[22] There is a progression through the verses from the opening plea for hearing, to the call in dire straits from the end of the earth, through the petition for safety, to the affirmation that God has served as a fortress against enemies. Verse 2 is a fervent plea for hearing. The pattern of each half of the verse is an imperative call to listen followed by the object with first common singular pronoun. The imperatives are of the longer, emphatic form, and the nouns are both singular. Verse 3 gives the petition greater focus, and v. 4 provides motivation for the plea. God has in the past afforded refuge; to do so again would bear witness to God's

---

[21]Our reading thus agrees with Muilenburg's suggestion that particles such as כִּי (vv. 4, 6) and כֵּן (v. 9) often mark the turning points in a text ("Particle כִּי," 135; "Form Criticism and Beyond," 14). Also note that אֱלֹהִים appears once in each section of the psalm (vv. 2, 6, 8).

[22]It is possible to treat v. 2 separately as introducing the entire psalm. Verse 3 does in some ways make a new beginning. However, commentators have seldom taken that position. Verse 3 continues the petition, in some ways making the introductory plea in v. 2 more specific. Our treatment will suggest additional ways in which vv. 2-4 belong together.

trustworthiness. The first common singular dominates, as subject of a verb אֶקְרָא "I call"; as the object of a verb תַּנְחֵנִי "lead me"; and as pronominal suffix:

רִנָּתִי	my cry
תְּפִלָּתִי	my prayer
לִבִּי	my heart
מִמֶּנִּי	from me
לִי	to me.

This preponderance also supports the unity of vv. 2-4. The section balances this use of the first common singular with second masculine singular imperatives in v. 2, שִׁמְעָה "Hear" and הַקְשִׁיבָה "Listen to;" the second masculine singular pronominal suffix in v. 3, אֵלֶיךָ "unto you;" and the second masculine singular verb in v. 4, הָיִיתָ "you have been." Note also the dominance of the *ḥîreq* (i) vowel sound in the verses, especially in the pausal forms. The sound of מ occurs seven times in the section. The similar sounds support the unity of vv. 2-4. In this section of the psalm, then, the speaker calls upon God for protection in the face of enemies and does so on the basis of past experience of God as strong fortress and refuge. Verse 4 provides motivation with כִּי for the prayer in vv. 2-3. So this section is plea followed by motivation, all addressed to אֱלֹהִים (v. 2).

II.

אָגוּרָה בְאָהָלְךָ עוֹלָמִים ⁵
אֶחֱסֶה בְסֵתֶר כְּנָפֶיךָ סֶּלָה:
כִּי־אַתָּה אֱלֹהִים שָׁמַעְתָּ לִנְדָרָי ⁶
נָתַתָּ יְרֻשַּׁת יִרְאֵי שְׁמֶךָ:

⁵Let me sojourn in your tent forever;
let me seek refuge in the shelter of your wings. Selah.
⁶Indeed, you, O God have heard my vows;
you have given the heritage of those who fear your name.

Verses 5-6 form the next section: v. 5 pleads for protection; v. 6 speaks of response to the plea. In this section, the second masculine singular dominates, with the suffix on בְאָהָלְךָ "in your tent" and כְּנָפֶיךָ "your wings" in v. 5 and on שְׁמֶךָ "your name" in v. 6 and with the second masculine singular verbs in v. 6: שָׁמַעְתָּ "you have heard" and נָתַתָּ "you have given." There is a sequence in these verses. The verbs in the petition in v. 5, in the imperfect, are first common singular followed by the preposition בְּ plus nouns with the second masculine singular suffix. In v. 6, the verbs, in the perfect, are second masculine singular; and the first one is followed by a noun with preposition and first common singular suffix: לִנְדָרַי. The second line of v. 6, however, concludes with the second masculine singular pronominal suffix on שְׁמֶךָ. The phrase is "those who fear your name." Clearly the speaker desires to be part of this group and so in a sense this phrase also refers to the speaker. Verses 5-6 serve to heighten the contrast between the speaker and the enemies mentioned at the end of v. 4. The two verses of this section provide good examples of poetic balance. Verse 5 has two lines with imperfect verb in the cohortative (אֶחֱסֶה, אָגוּרָה) followed by the preposition בְּ with object. Typically the parallel is more of an echo than an exact synonym:

אָגוּרָה בְאָהָלְךָ עוֹלָמִים
Let me dwell in your tent forever;
אֶחֱסֶה בְסֵתֶר כְּנָפֶיךָ
let me seek refuge in the shelter of your wings.

The same holds for v. 6. The two parts indicate that God has heard and God has given, but the emphasis is on the subject in the first part of the verse: "for you, God, have heard" (כִּי־אַתָּה אֱלֹהִים שָׁמַעְתָּ) "my vows" (לִנְדָרַי). In the second half of the verse, the emphasis is on the object יְרֻשַּׁת יִרְאֵי שְׁמֶךָ, "the heritage of those who fear your name," which God has given (נָתַתָּ). This section of the psalm also moves the focus clearly to the temple, with reference to "your tent" (בְאָהָלְךָ) and "the shadow of your wings" (בְסֵתֶר כְּנָפֶיךָ) as well as the vows (לִנְדָרַי) that are performed in the temple cult.

Verse 6 raises some difficult issues. I have taken the verse, in line with most commentators, as an expression of certainty; God has heard the worshipper's prayer. The emphatic beginning of the verse, כִּי־אַתָּה אֱלֹהִים שָׁמַעְתָּ, would indicate such, especially in response to שִׁמְעָה אֱלֹהִים in v. 2. This interpretation takes כִּי in its deictic sense.[23] The

---

[23]See Muilenburg, "Particle כִּי," 136.

beginning of v. 6 corresponds to other expressions of certainty in the Psalms (Pss 6:9-11; 28:6-7; 31:22-23; 55:17-20). The shift to an expression of certainty might explain the location of סֶלָה at the conclusion of v. 5.[24] The difficulty is that what God hears is vows. One would expect a word for prayer, such as תְּפִלָּתִי or רִנָּתִי (v. 2). Vows were associated with prayers; does the term imply accompanying prayers?[25] Or does the statement imply that God answered the prayer of the speaker who, in consequence, has already made vows in God's hearing? The second part of the verse also raises the question of the significance of יְרֻשַּׁת, "heritage," if we are to retain the MT and if that is the proper translation of the word. To this question we will return in chapter three. Verse 6 does, however, provide transition to the third verse paragraph of our psalm. The heritage given at the end of v. 6 leads to the petition for the guarantor of that heritage, the king, in vv. 7-8. Also note the use of "your name" (שְׁמֶךָ and שִׁמְךָ) and "vows" (לִנְדָרֶי and נְדָרֵי) in vv. 6 and 9, respectively.

To sum up, vv. 5-6 are petition followed by an expression of the certainty of a hearing. The prayer in v. 5 seeks protection in the temple and inclusion among the faithful; v. 6 speaks of response.

III.

יָמִים עַל־יְמֵי־מֶלֶךְ תּוֹסִיף ⁷
שְׁנוֹתָיו כְּמוֹ־דֹר וָדֹר:
יֵשֵׁב עוֹלָם לִפְנֵי אֱלֹהִים ⁸
חֶסֶד וֶאֱמֶת מַן יִנְצְרֻהוּ:
כֵּן אֲזַמְּרָה שִׁמְךָ לָעַד ⁹

---

[24]On the various ways to explain the sudden change of mood in the laments from crisis to hope, see W. H. Bellinger, Jr., *Psalmody and Prophecy*, JSOTSup 27 (Sheffield: JSOT Press, 1984) 78-82; T. W. Cartledge, "Conditional Vows in the Psalms of Lament: A New Approach to an Old Problem," *The Listening Heart: Essays in Wisdom and the Psalms in Honor of Roland E. Murphy, O. Carm.*, ed. Kenneth G. Hoglund, Elizabeth F. Huwiler, Johnathan T. Glass, and Roger W. Lee, JSOTSup 58 (Sheffield: Sheffield Academic Press, 1987) 77-94.

[25]The versions seem to provide support for that view. See Patrick Boylan, *The Psalms: A Study of the Vulgate in the Light of the Hebrew Text* (Dublin: M. H. Gill and Sons Ltd., 1920–1924) 222.

לְשַׁלְמִי נְדָרַי יוֹם יוֹם:

[7]Add days upon days for the king,
his years as generation after generation.
[8]Let him be enthroned forever before God;
appoint loyalty and trustworthiness to watch over him.
[9]Thus I will praise your name forever
as I fulfil my vows day by day.

Verses 7-9 form the final verse paragraph of the psalm. The section is set off with clear markers, the references to "days upon days" beginning v. 7 and "day by day" to conclude v. 9. This section also begins with petition in vv. 7-8. The verbs are imperfect, and the sequence is noun followed by verbs in the first part of v. 7; the second half of the verse has no verb. In v. 8, the sequence is verb followed by noun and then the reverse in the second half of the verse. Each verse seems to have a progression: from days to years to generations in v. 7; from enthronement to protection by God's חֶסֶד וֶאֱמֶת in v. 8; from praise forever to fulfilling vows daily in v. 9. The sound of מ (m) occurs thirteen times in this section. Verse 9 exhibits some parallels to v. 6 with the hearing and fulfilling of vows. Verse 8 also speaks of protection for the king as v. 5 does for the speaker. Note the use of עוֹלָם in v. 8 and עוֹלָמִים in v. 5.

The psalm seems to intensify and look back as it comes to its end, marked by the concluding כֵּן. Here the emphasis is on the acts of the speaker: praise and the fulfilling of vows. Note the use of the first common singular as the subject of a verb, אֲזַמְּרָה, "I will sing," and the first common singular suffixes in the second half of the verse: לְשַׁלְמִי נְדָרַי, "as I fulfil my vows." The praise is offered to שִׁמְךָ, "your name." The entire psalm has a hopeful tone and concludes that way as well. Verse 9 includes balanced lines of verb followed by object with a reference to time; the praise and completion of vows is to continue. This last section of the psalm also pictures the speaker as a faithful worshiper. The fulfillment of vows and the praise of God go on through life. In that life, vv. 7-8 petition for protection of the king and extension of his rule. This section extends the earlier parts of the psalm to the community and to the future.[26]

Psalm 61 thus consists of three sections: vv. 2-4 as petition followed by motivation, vv. 5-6 as petition followed by an expression of the certainty of a hearing, and vv. 7-9 as petition followed by vow.

This description of structure is, however, not the only possibility for Psalm 61. A simpler description of structure would be that proposed by Delitzsch and Kirkpatrick as noted above. The first part of the psalm voices prayer (vv. 2-5) and the last part of the text expresses confidence (vv. 6-9). We could consider v. 5 with vv. 2-4. It continues the plea for protection and the root חָסָה occurs in v. 4 and in v. 5. The location of סֶלָה at the end of v. 5 also offers support. We have also already noted the connections between v. 6 and what follows, especially v. 9. This proposal also has the advantages of simplicity and clarity. The disadvantages appear primarily in v. 6 and v. 7. The beginning of v. 6, כִּי־אַתָּה אֱלֹהִים שָׁמַעְתָּ, refers back to שָׁמְעָה אֱלֹהִים in v. 1. Separating v. 6 from what precedes would ignore the structural marker. In addition, treating vv. 6-9 together ignores the *inclusio* setting off vv. 7-9: יָמִים עַל־יְמֵי (v. 7) and יוֹם יוֹם (v. 9).

Another viable alternative is to leave the structure as vv. 2-4/5-6/7-9 but to describe the middle section differently. We have already noted the difficulties with v. 6. The verse could be interpreted not as an expression of certainty that God has heard the prayer but as motivation following the prayer in v. 5 (note the quote from A. A. Anderson that began our discussion of structure). Vows could provide motivation for God to answer prayer. The granting of the "heritage" in the last half of the verse could also refer to God's past actions. Thus the verse would provide motivation to answer the prayer in v. 5 in the same way that v. 4 does for the petition in vv. 2-3. Verses 2-6 would then make up a double petition, each followed by motivation. The interpretation of the pivotal v. 6 is problematic, but its beginning does give the appearance of an expression of certainty that God has heard. The latter half of the verse also seems to reflect response to the prayer. Such are the disadvantages of this reading.

---

[26]It would be possible to treat v. 9 separately as the conclusion to the entire psalm, but such a move would ignore the *inclusio* setting off vv. 7-9.

A final possible structure for Psalm 61 is that outlined by A. A. Anderson and Kraus above. It is essentially the same structure proposed by Gunkel. Gunkel, however, suggested that vv. 7-8 are a later addition to the psalm. Our discussion of structure above would argue against that view, given the *inclusio* which we have seen marks off vv. 7-9 and the relationships we noted between v. 5 and v. 8. The proposal of structure, however, does not depend on the secondary nature of vv. 7-8. Rather, it concentrates on traditional form-critical terms and gives little emphasis to poetic devices. Verses 2-3 are petition; vv. 4-5 express trust and a wish; v. 6 expresses the certainty of a hearing; vv. 7-8 intercede for the king; and v. 9 voices the vow. We have already noted connections between v. 4 and v. 5. Verse 4 (with כִּי) could certainly introduce a request, though the causal motivation most often follows the petition.[27] This final suggestion for the structure of the psalm attempts to clarify the function of the various parts of the poem; the location of סֶלָה at the end of v. 5 also provides support. This proposal is certainly a viable alternative. Its disadvantage, however, is that it ignores the markers setting off vv. 7-9 and vv. 2-6, as well as the poetic devices which suggest that vv. 2-4 are a unity. We have also noted unifying elements in vv. 5-6.

Our first proposal for the structure of Psalm 61 appears to be preferable. However, all four proposals have advantages. Certainty is not possible. The features the various proposals emphasize are all in the text. Thus poetic ambiguity comes to the fore. A full reading of Psalm 61 will not choose only one structural reading. Rather, the interpreter becomes aware that each proposal offers an angle of vision which may help unlock the significance of the psalm.[28] Our work has already shown that various readings of Psalm 61 are plausible. Each reading contributes to the task of interpretation. In this sense, ambiguity is positive. Our discussion of the psalm from this point on must consider the various readings. How-

---

[27]BDB, 473.

[28]For a study that is keenly aware of the ambiguity in the text, see Pierre Auffret, "Essai sur la structure literaire de Psaume 61," *JANES* 14 (1982): 1-10. Auffret's essay reflects a structuralist theory of reading texts. I suspect, however, that his view is very complicated for readers, ancient or modern. His later treatment of the psalm seems a bit less complicated (" 'ALORS JE JOURERAI SANS FIN POUR TON NOM' Etude structurelle du psaume 61," *Science et Esprit* 36 [1984]: 169-77).

ever, I have suggested a primary interpretation, and what follows will give special attention to that view.

In summary, that interpretation understands Psalm 61 as a petition with three sections (vv. 2-4, 5-6, 7-9). To put it a little differently, v. 2 introduces the theme of the prayer with a cry for help. Verses 3, 5, 7-8 extend the plea, primarily in terms of protection, while v. 4 gives motivation for God to respond favorably to the petition in vv. 2-3. The motivation is put in terms of God's past actions. Verse 6 reflects God's positive response to the prayer. The psalm also concludes on a positive note in v. 9 with a vow of praise. Verses 7-9 give the prayer a wider community reference. The psalm is thus a classic example of a plea for protection.

The Genre

Our examination of Psalm 61 leads to the conclusion that it should be considered as representative of the genre of individual laments or complaints.[29] The psalm is not a thanksgiving psalm; the crisis is still present, though more implicitly than explicitly. Neither does the psalm fit well with the trust psalms, though the prayer does have a confident tone. Plea dominates, but the prayer is not a "God lament," to use the terms of Broyles.[30] The psalm operates out of expectation that God will hear and answer and provide protection. So, to be more specific, Psalm 61 is a plea or petition or prayer, תְּפִלָּה, for protection within the

---

[29]For a brief description of the genre or *Gattung*, see Bellinger, *Psalmody and Prophecy*, 22-24. I have retained the traditional term "lament," though the text is not a dirge, a cry of resignation. It is rather a plea for help. Thus, Gerstenberger would prefer the term "complaint." See Erhard S. Gerstenberger, *Psalms: Part I with an Introduction to Cultic Poetry*, FOTL 14 (Grand Rapids: Eerdmans, 1988) 10-14. Westermann might suggest that the psalm is a petition that has been heard; see Claus Westermann, *Praise and Lament in the Psalms* (Atlanta: John Knox Press, 1981) 80.

[30]Broyles, *Conflict of Faith and Experience*.

classification "individual lament."[31] It relates to temple and king; further comment will come in the next chapter.

Conclusion

This chapter has explored Psalm 61 as an individual lament. We have noted various proposals for the structure of the psalm and will need to consider these in our further approaches to the text. We must now move to the other major concern of form criticism, the *Sitz im Leben*.

---

[31]See Gunkel and Begrich, *Einleitung*, 249, 259. This description of the genre leans heavily on translating the psalm in terms of petition (see the appendix, below). If one construes the verbs primarily in terms of indicative statements of confidence, the prayer is moved toward trust. After the introductory plea, the speaker expresses profound confidence in God. Seen that way, the psalm would be a psalm of confidence or protective psalm. I take genre to be a matter of classification as opposed to some sort of normative decision which limits the further interpretation of the psalm. A genre classification provides the interpreter with a broader base of study—comparison with other texts of similar genre. One must be careful not to draw too rigidly the lines between categories. Psalms of lament, thanksgiving, and trust have a number of similarities. See the helpful studies in J. H. Hayes, *Old Testament Form Criticism* (San Antonio TX: Trinity University Press, 1974); M. J. Buss, "The Study of Forms," in *Encounter with the Text: Form and History in the Hebrew Bible*, ed. Buss, *Semeia* supplements (Philadelphia: Fortress Press; Missoula MT: Scholars Press, 1979) 1-56; E. Gerstenberger, *Psalms*, 179-223; and R. Knierim, "Old Testament Form Criticism Reconsidered," *Int* 27 (1973): 435-68. Broyles, *Conflict of Faith and Experience*, 22-27, provides helpful comments on the definition of genre; his approach reflects an informed view of form criticism. Perhaps the current setting of the speaker would determine which view of the psalm prevailed. See John Goldingay, "If Your Sins Are like Scarlet (Isaiah 1:18)," *StTh* 35 (1981): 137-44. Goldingay's concluding comments relate to contemporary application of the text, but they could also be relevant to its use in ancient Israel.

Setting

Introduction

The form-critical task begins with establishing the unit for analysis, exploring structure, and determining genre; it continues by exploring the *Sitz im Leben* from which the text derives. The method concentrates on the typical, and suggests that genres come from discernible settings in the social and religious life of communities. Hymns derive from worship; alphabet practice tablets derive from schools. These introductory comments illustrate some of the difficulties with terminology.[1] *Sitz im Leben* connotes at least three aspects of the background of a text: the social/religious institution from which the text derives, where the text fits in that institution, and the text's broad social matrix. Our discussion will attempt to clarify each of these aspects.

Again, the text invites the reader to ask such questions. Our psalm refers to "the end of the earth," "the enemy," God's "tent," the shelter of God's "wings," "the king," "vows," and "praise." Some other psalms are even more explicit with references to altars, processions, and temple. To what did these terms refer? From what place in the life of ancient Israel did Psalm 61 derive? Dealing with such questions may help the reader fill in gaps so as to better appropriate the text. A number of proposals have been made in attempts to account for the origin of our psalm.

---

[1]See Douglas A Knight, "The Understanding of 'Sitz im Leben' in Form Criticism," SBLSP 1 (1974): 105-25; Martin J. Buss, "The Idea of Sitz im Leben—History and Critique," *ZAW* 90 (1978): 157-70. Our treatment of Psalm 61 should give expression to the text's mental matrix or major concern; see R. Knierem, "Old Testament Form Criticism Reconsidered," 435-68.

The Personal/Historical Approach

A number of studies prior to the advent of form criticism sought the origin of psalms in the life of a particular person or in an event in the history of ancient Israel. They then interpreted the psalm in light of that background. Scholars engaged in such a quest were seeking a personal or historical event as a setting (in the narrowest sense) from which a psalm derived.

One of the more extreme proposals for the setting of Psalm 61, in this approach, came from Moses Buttenwieser.[2] He arranged his commentary on the Psalms in chronological order and placed his comment on Psalm 61 in the collection of psalms deriving from the postexilic period, more specifically from 318–312 B.C.E. He suggests that the psalm bears similarity to other texts he dates from that period (Pss. 55; 56; 57; 59; 142) and that it reflects the difficulties from those years following the death of Alexander the Great. Buttenwieser eliminates vv. 7-8 from consideration because he asserts that these verses have been misplaced from Psalm 72. On the basis of v. 3, he understands the psalm's speaker to be on the country's frontier in a time of national jeopardy. The speaker has either fled before the invader or been taken prisoner with other Judeans prior to Ptolemy's siege of Jerusalem.

A view more characteristic of the personal/historical approach would be that of A. F. Kirkpatrick.[3] He also suggests that the speaker is far from Jerusalem and, given the royal associations of the text, that the psalm came from the life of David. The best possibility is during the time at Mahanaim when Absalom's revolt was over but David had not returned to the capital city. The king longs to be in his city. The heritage given (v. 6) is the land still granted to David and his followers, for the king's life is no longer in danger (v. 7). Thus the setting in David's life issues in the confidence reflected in the psalm. Eventually the text came to be interpreted in terms of the Messiah.

---

[2]Moses Buttenwieser, *The Psalms Chronologically Treated with a New Translation* (Chicago: University of Chicago Press, 1938) 756-58.

[3]Kirkpatrick, *Psalms*, 344-47.

Another notable alternative of the personal/historical kind is the view of Barnes that the king involved is Jehoiachin in captivity in Babylon.[4] The psalm thus has to do with the difficulties of the years 597-587 B.C.E. The speaker is also in exile and hopes to return to Jerusalem with the king. The psalm is a restrained one so as not to alarm the Babylonian captors.

The interpretations from a personal/historical perspective attempt to fill in the psalm's gaps in order to help the reader relate the psalm to real life. However, the approach has been discarded by scholarship because of the language in the Psalms. The language is of a much more representative or typical kind. Form criticism has clearly noted the typical features of the Psalms and looks for a setting for such features. So while the views of Buttenwieser, Kirkpatrick, and Barnes provide intelligible readings of Psalm 61, the general nature of the psalm's language makes it impossible to settle on a specific personal/historical setting as the key for interpretation. Nothing in the text provides sufficient evidence for the specific date of the psalm or its background in the life of an individual. That approach certainly does not reveal the "original" meaning of the text in ancient Israel. A more promising approach is the cultic one.

Cultic Approaches

The form-critical work of Hermann Gunkel provided the way forward out of the personal/historical morass.[5] Form criticism understands genre in terms of that which is typical and so looks for a *Sitz im Leben* from which such a genre might have originated. Gunkel and others after him understood the psalms' genres to have come from the institution of worship. The individual laments generally reflect a setting of crisis described as a sojourn in Sheol, the realm of death. The power of death has invaded life and, in some way, diminished wholeness for the speaker who seeks God's help through cultic prayer.[6] References to temple and worship, crisis and enemy certainly support such a background for Psalm 61.

---

[4]W. E. Barnes, *The Psalms*, WC (London: Methuen & Co., 1931) 288.
[5]On the methodological issues, see Bellinger, *Psalms*, 15-32.
[6]See Bellinger, *Psalms*, 44-73.

The somewhat different approach of Othmar Keel provides additional information on the cultic background of our text.[7] Through his study of ancient Near Eastern iconography as it relates to the Psalms, Keel suggests that מִקְצֵה הָאָרֶץ, "the end of the earth," in v. 3 indicates the edge of chaos, the place of surrender to the power of death. In contrast, the temple is the locus of life. It is like a strong defensive tower; it provides protection under God's wings and signifies the sheltering sky. The wings may also allude to the cherubim in the holy of holies and to the protection of the young under a bird's wings. Keel's suggestions accord well with our description of the general setting of the laments.

In broad terms, then, the situation of the speaker in Psalm 61 is similar to that of other laments. The person is gripped by the power of death, experiencing a sojourn in Sheol.[8] Can we be more specific about the cultic *Sitz im Leben* of our psalm?

General Cultic Settings. Gunkel's treatment of Psalm 61 is rather general.[9] The speaker seeks protection in the sanctuary. While Gunkel considers vv. 7-8 an addition to the psalm, those verses indicate that the psalm, including that addition, comes from the time of the monarchy. Verses 7-8 relate to king, temple, and Jerusalem. The speaker wishes to make pilgrimage to the Jerusalem temple. Schmidt suggests that the speaker of the text may be sick and thus prays in worship,[10] and Anderson gives a rather general cultic interpretation of the psalm.[11]

A Psalm of Thanksgiving. Artur Weiser offers a different cultic interpretation.[12] He understands the psalm as an expression of thanksgiving

---

[7]Othmar Keel, *The Symbolism of the Biblical World: Ancient Near Eastern Iconography and the Book of Psalms*, trans. Timothy J. Hallett (New York: Seabury, 1978) 24-25, 28-29, 39, 112, 118, 163, 180-81, 190-92. See also Marvin E. Tate, *Psalms 51-100*, WBC 20 (Dallas: Word Books, 1990) 114.

[8]This statement would be true whether we consider Psalm 61 as a prayer of lament or a psalm of confidence.

[9]Gunkel, *Psalmen*, 260-62.

[10]Schmidt, *Psalmen*, 116-17.

[11]Anderson, *Psalms*, 1:446-50.

[12]Weiser, *Psalms*, 442-45. Weiser's view needs to be seen in light of the debate over Mowinckel's proposal of a fall enthronement festival, Weiser's suggestion of a covenant festival, and Kraus's reconstruction of a Royal-Zion Festival. See Clements, *A Century of Old Testament Study*, 76-95, for a summary.

after the petition has been fulfilled. The recitation takes place in the covenant renewal festival. Weiser's reconstruction of the festival from the Pentateuch includes a ritual distribution of land, and he suggests this occasion as the one on which the thanksgiving psalm was recited. The speaker has been granted a piece of land, and this event confirms that God has favorably heard the prayer. Alternatively, the worshiper has been granted assurance of God's hearing the prayer and associates that with the granting of land. The speaker thus gives thanks to God. The king guarantees the observance and execution of the ritual decision. Thus the petitioner prays for the king, the guarantor of the possession of land. The association with the king shows the psalm's significance for the whole community, and the cultic setting shows the intricate relation between life and worship in ancient Israel.

Weiser's view provides a legitimate means of accounting for the prayer for the king in Psalm 61 and makes sense of the last part of v. 6. However, I find it unlikely that the prayer is a psalm of thanksgiving; the crisis seems still to be present. In addition, Weiser's reconstruction of the covenant renewal festival, and especially his suggestion of a setting for so many psalms in it, has not found a wide following.

A Prayer for Asylum. H.-J. Kraus's interpretation of the psalm has affinities with the notion of asylum.[13] The speaker is pursued by enemies and seeks the shelter of the temple and city of the divine presence. The person receives a favorable hearing (v. 6). Kraus also suggests that petition for the king may have been a part of prayers used in the sanctuary; so vv. 7-8 fit the Jerusalem temple tradition. Kraus's description of the shelter of the holy place is reminiscent of Keel's view of the significance of the sanctuary.[14] This view holds promise but is still quite general.

---

[13]Kraus, *Psalms 60-150,* 7-10. Kraus's view is similar to Gunkel's but moves in a certain direction. Kraus's view also has affinities with Weiser's in that asylum has been granted; the hope is that the protection will continue.

[14]See above. Anthropological studies, especially of relevant Pentateuchal texts, also contribute to the conversation. See, e.g., Bernhard Lang, ed., *Anthropological Approaches to the Old Testament,* IRT 8 (Philadelphia: Fortress Press, 1985); Frank H. Gorman, Jr., *The Ideology of Ritual: Space, Time and Status in the Priestly Theology,* JSOTSup 91 (Sheffield: Sheffield Academic Press, 1990).

A related but rather different cultic interpretation of the psalm comes from Lienhard Delekat.[15] He understands many of the individual laments as inscriptions, analogous to those in Egypt, left in the temple as pleas for asylum. The petitioners await word from God on their request occasioned by their being persecuted by creditors or accusers. The expressions of certainty were added to the psalms later when God had granted the petitioner either safe passage or a position as a temple servant. He compares Psalm 61 to Psalm 84 and suggests that the king was the guarantor of the asylum expected in Psalm 61. Difficulties abound in Delekat's proposal. He places too many psalms in this one setting, and the laments are psalms rather than inscriptions; the two are not the same. His interpretations are often strained at best when dealing with the particulars of psalms.[16]

Royal Interpretations. Several scholars have suggested that the speaker in Psalm 61 is the king in the midst of crisis. This suggestion relates to the wider issue of how many of the Psalms are Royal Psalms. This question goes back to the old problem of the identification of the "I" of the Psalms. Also relevant is the identification of the enemies in the laments. Some have suggested that the adversaries are national enemies and that the speaker is thus the national leader, the king.[17]

Also part of the background of this issue is the question of whether there was a "royal ritual" in Jerusalem. Aubrey Johnson, in particular, has suggested that there was such a temple ritual and that a part of it was the ritual humiliation of the king.[18] The king, representative of the people, was humiliated in a ritual battle and then restored to celebrate God's victory over the powers of chaos and renewal of creation. Psalms of lament could have served as prayers in that ritual.

---

[15]Lienhard Delekat, *Asylie und Schutzorakel am Zionheiligtum* (Leiden: E. J. Brill, 1967).

[16]Deissler interprets the psalm as the prayer of a Levite and thus one who will in fact stay in the temple: Deissler, *Die Psalmen*, 2:237-39.

[17]See Bellinger, *Psalmody and Prophecy*, 28-31; and J. H. Eaton, "The Psalms and Israelite Worship," in *Tradition and Interpretation*, ed. G. W. Anderson (Oxford: Clarendon Press, 1979) 238-73, on the history of the issue.

[18]Aubrey R. Johnson, *Sacral Kingship in Ancient Israel* (Cardiff: University of Wales Press, 1955). Also see Aage Bentzen, *King and Messiah*, LSCB (London: Lutterworth, 1955).

The British scholar John Eaton has provided notable support for the royal interpretation of many psalms.[19] He traces the history of scholarship on the issue and examines other attempts to find a *Sitz im Leben* for the individual laments. He judges these other attempts to fail. Eaton calls on the associations of David with the Psalter and the importance of the king in ancient Israel as a means of offering an alternative royal interpretation of the laments. In these psalms, the enemies are national ones, and the king represents the people in prayer to God as a part of the king's special relationship with God. This interpretation conforms to the ancient Near Eastern understanding of kingship. It also enables one to see these psalms as meaningful wholes. Otherwise, the royal elements in them are problematic.

Eaton places Psalm 61 among those he considers to be clearly royal. Psalm 61 mentions the king in vv. 7-8, and Eaton suggests that it is most natural to understand the speaker who moves to confidence and thanksgiving to be the king himself. The change to the third person is to emphasize the king's gift of abundant life and to echo the people's prayer for the king (v. 6).

> That the psalmist is indeed the king is further indicated by his exaltation
> and his finding a fortress in God (vv. 3f., . . .) his everlasting sojourn
> in God's tent, sheltering under God's wings (v. 5, . . .) and his vow of
> daily sacrifices with music for ever (v. 9, . . .).[20]

Eaton understands the psalm as a prayer of confidence from the king who faces the mouth of Sheol but who is led by God to a high rock, a reference suggestive of the king's enthronement on Zion after processional ascent. The psalm concentrates on the king's close relationship with God. The king's rule and sojourn in God's protection under fidelity and truth (v. 8) will be eternal. God has heard the prayers and vows offered for the king. The king bears witness to trust in God.

Eaton suggests that the background of this royal prayer is a battle setting, presumably in the royal ritual, though his comments on that are not

---

[19]J. H. Eaton, *Kingship and the Psalms*, SBT 2nd ser. 32 (London: SCM Press, 1976) esp. 47-49. The 2nd ed. of Eaton's volume (The Biblical Seminar [Sheffield: JSOT, 1986]) provides a helpful survey of recent contributions to the issue (221-40) but no real change in his argument.

[20]Eaton, *Kingship and the Psalms*, 48.

altogether clear.[21] The psalm also reflects several of the ideals of the king's office: the king's presence in God's aura (v. 8), God's gift of abundant life (vv. 7-8), assistance by the personified covenant-graces (v. 8), and the king's witness to the world (v. 9).[22]

In his earlier commentary, Eaton also argued that Psalm 61 is royal (note that English versification is used):

> This is best taken throughout as the prayer of a Davidic King from a situation of great distress. He changes from the first to the third person in vv. 6-7, a common oriental idiom used, for example, by King Zedekiah in Jer. 38.5. The effect here is to invoke God's promises to the king as such (cf. 18.50); also perhaps to echo the traditional blessing-wish made over the king by the community (see on v. 5b). It is fairly obvious that the king's need forms the single theme running right through the psalm; note especially the vow of daily offerings in v. 8. While some take v. 2 to indicate that he is on some distant campaign or travelling to answer charges before an overlord, others take the reference more figuratively; the question resembles that raised by Pss. 42/3.[23]

Johnson's treatment of Psalm 61 came in his last published volume. He considers the prayer a royal psalm and the setting also as the danger of slipping into the mouth of Sheol.[24] The prayer is spoken by a cult prophet on behalf of the king. The hope is that the king will not continue to be pulled down in Sheol but will continue to live under God's guidance as a part of the community of faith. The psalm refers to the king's faithfulness and associates that with a long life. The specific setting of the text is difficult to determine because the psalm's wording is so general, but illness and war have been suggested. Johnson even suggests that the psalm could have come from the early days of David and Nathan.

A recent study has also examined the royal interpretation of the Psalms. Steven J. L. Croft considers again the question of the "I" of the

---

[21]See Eaton, *Kingship and the Psalms*, 131.

[22]These comments indicate the circular nature of Eaton's argument. Suggestions of the royal ideal confirm the royal nature of psalms, and yet the evidence for that royal ideal comes from the psalms.

[23]Eaton, *Psalms*, 156-57.

[24]Aubrey R. Johnson, *The Cultic Prophet and Israel's Psalmody* (Cardiff: University of Wales Press, 1979) 97-98, 352-59.

Psalms.[25] He treats the question of the identity in the Psalms of the enemies, the poor, and the individual as king, private person, and cultic minister. He takes a constructive approach, understanding that the Psalter is a diverse book and that one solution to a problem such as the identity of the individual will not fit all the texts. He surveys the history of scholarship on the subject and spends a good deal of time on Eaton's position. He criticizes Eaton for seeking one solution to a complex problem, for mixing arguments which dispose one to a royal interpretation of psalms and those which give evidence that a particular psalm is royal, and for a lack of attention to the setting of "royal" psalms which were not part of the royal temple ritual. Arguments which dispose one to interpret a number of psalms as royal include the importance of the king in ancient Israel's life, the presence elsewhere in the Old Testament of the setting of royal prayers, the gap left in ancient Israel's royal prayer literature if a number of the laments are not from the king (other ancient Near Eastern nations had such), and the presence of לְדָוִד, "Of David," in so many psalm superscriptions. Arguments which speak for a specific psalm as royal include mention of the king, a royal *Sitz im Leben* for the text, and "royal style."

Croft suggests that Eaton's description of "royal style" is not sufficient to determine the matter. The style could have been democratized, that is, modified to apply to persons other than the king; elements of the style occur in nonroyal psalms; and the reasoning is circular. Psalms are used to determine the elements of a royal style, and then the presence of that style becomes evidence for classifying a psalm as royal. Unfortunately, Croft does not escape this problem, for he insists on speaking of a royal style with reference to divine epithets.

The particular shape of the Jerusalem royal festival then becomes Croft's focus of attention. The ritual is commonly described as including a time of preparation, the procession with the ark, ritual combat and humiliation, entering the temple, enthronement of the king, and God's judgment on the wicked. Croft rejects the arguments of Johnson and Eaton for a ritual of royal humiliation. Such a setting is not attested elsewhere in the Old Testament, and psalms related to it may just as well reflect a

---

[25]Steven J. L. Croft, *The Identity of the Individual in the Psalms*, JSOTSup 44 (Sheffield: JSOT Press, 1987).

situation of actual battle. In addition, Croft argues that the Babylonian texts produced to support the ritual of humiliation are not analogous to the relevant psalms. Croft's reconstruction of the royal festival includes preparation in which the king is declared innocent and renewed, procession and ritual battle, confirmation of the king and the judgment of God. Psalms recited by the king and by others come in this last category. Croft goes on to discuss royal psalms not used in the festival, but rather in times of war, need, assurance, or a royal wedding (Ps. 45).

According to Croft, Psalm 61 fits the category of a prayer recited in the royal festival by someone speaking on behalf of the king. Croft gives little space specifically to our text; but he notes that it contains an intercession for the king in the third person, similar to that in Psalm 72. The first part of Psalm 61 contains several examples of "royal style," and Croft suggests that the entire psalm is probably royal. The psalm is set in the last part of the festival confirming the king, who looks back to prayers already answered (v. 5) and forward to new dangers (v. 3).

The argument really hinges on how one accounts for the explicit mention of the king. I have already questioned the notion of a "royal style," elements of which are precious few in Psalm 61;[26] and we have already seen various suggestions of a setting for the psalm. I have elsewhere chronicled the difficulties of a royal interpretation of many laments.[27] A full explication is not necessary. However, the primary points may be helpful in the discussion. I take the relationship between the Davidic king and the psalms more in terms of patron than in terms of the actual subject of the text. The arguments for the view that the enemies in the individual laments are national enemies also do not hold promise. A more constructive approach begins with the view that the relationship between individual and community was a fluid one in ancient Israel. In addition, does the presence of "royal elements" make a psalm a Royal Psalm? The Psalter was put together after the fall of the Davidic monarchy. It is surprising that there are Royal Psalms included; no doubt some are there by way of a messianic interpretation. There may well have been a royal festival in Jerusalem, perhaps even a royal ritual of hu-

---

[26]See Croft, *Identity of the Individual*, 78-80.

[27]Bellinger, *Psalmody and Prophecy*, 28-31; and *Psalms*, 106-23.

miliation involving Royal Psalms. I doubt, however, that many individual laments derived from that setting.

Psalm 61, however, explicitly mentions the king. For that reason, while the royal interpretation of Psalm 61 is far from established, it must be considered as a real possibility. It accounts for the presence of the intercession for the king.[28] The proposals of Gunkel, Weiser, Kraus, and Delekat all seek to account for that prayer in some way. In many ways, the issue comes down to one's view of the temple cult. Was it a royal cult, or more open to public participation? Further comment will come shortly.[29]

A Proposal. Our survey of the various options for the setting of Psalm 61 suggests that several elements of the psalm need to be considered when making a proposal. The psalm, first of all, is a psalm seeking help; the particular help centers on safety and protection (vv. 2-5). The sanctuary is also at the heart of the psalm's concern (vv. 5-6, 9). The question of the significance of יְרֻשַּׁת, "heritage," in v. 6 also enters the picture, as does the prayer for the king (vv. 7-8). We need to consider all these factors when reconstructing the psalm's setting.

Some sort of protection related to the temple does seem to be in the background of Psalm 61. We have noted the possibility of a rite of asylum. An institution of asylum is well attested in the Old Testament.[30] The asylum was of two forms—in the sanctuary or at the altar (Exod. 21:12-14; 1 Kings 1:50; 2:28) and in the cities of refuge (Num. 35; Deut. 4:41-43; 19:1ff.; Josh. 20). The passages cited relate to the law of homicide.

---

[28]According to Tate, "The view that the psalm contains a prayer *for* the king is equally as probable as the conclusion that it is a prayer by a king" (*Psalms 51-100*, 112).

[29]Other scholars have also identified Psalm 61 as royal. See Dahood, *Psalms*, 2:83-88; Mowinckel, *The Psalms in Israel's Worship*, 1:48-49, 220, 226, 242. Mowinckel, who is perhaps the prime instigator of much cultic interpretation of the Psalms, understands the psalm "as a prayer accompanying the offerings before the battle, far away from that capital and Temple which the king hopes to see again before long" (226). As such the psalm is among the "protective psalms," emphasizing a note of confidence in God's protection prior to the battle. These "protective psalms" are among what Mowinckel calls the "national congregational laments in the I-form."

[30]See Bellinger, *Psalmody and Prophecy*, 47-50.

After a homicide, the killer faced death automatically, in line with the custom of blood vengeance. However, the killer could seek asylum in order to prove that the killing was accidental and thus to stop the shedding of innocent blood. Perhaps at an early period the asylum was at the sanctuary and later at the city of refuge. Perhaps the cities had a tradition associating them with sanctuaries.[31] The killer would then present the case and, if found innocent, be granted asylum. If found guilty, execution was at hand (Lev. 24:12; Num. 15:32-36). The asylum was apparently temporary and an attempt to ensure justice.

The passages we have noted deal with the problem of unintentional manslaughter; could the practice of asylum apply to a wider variety of acts? That is certainly possible, though the Old Testament is simply silent on the subject. But was the right of asylum actually practiced in ancient Israel? The texts describing the institution are late; but the descriptions have all the marks of an early institution, if not always in the advanced form in Numbers, Deuteronomy, and Joshua.[32] As I have noted, several commentators on the psalms have seen asylum as the background of psalms.[33]

Is Psalm 61 a prayer for asylum? The text is a plea for protection and safety (vv. 2-3, 5). It clearly has associations with the temple with בְאָהָלְךָ, "in your tent," and בְּסֵתֶר כְּנָפֶיךָ, "in the shadow of your wings," in v. 5, and with the vows and praise in vv. 6, 9. So it would appear that the sanctuary is the locus of protection because of God's presence there and that the prayer is for some form of asylum. The

---

[31]See N. M. Nicolsky, "Das Asylrecht in Israel," *ZAW* 48 (1930): 146-75; Moshe Greenberg, "The Biblical Conception of Asylum," *JBL* 78 (1959): 125-32. J. Milgrom, "Sancta Contagion and Altar/City Asylum," *Congress Volume, Vienna 1980*, VTSup 32 (Leiden: E. J. Brill, 1981) 278-310, argues that the practice of altar asylum no longer existed after the early monarchy. City asylum in Priestly and Deuteronomic texts serves the function of moving the evil (killing) involved away from the holy altar. Thus the cities of refuge were not considered sanctuaries.

[32]See H. McKeating, "The Development of the Law on Homicide in Ancient Israel," *VT* 25 (1975): 53-56.

[33]See Edward Westermarck, "Asylum," *Encyclopedia of Religion and Ethics*, ed. James Hastings (Edinburgh: T. & T. Clark, 1909) 2:161-64, for a description of the practice of asylum among other cultures.

psalm, however, gives no indication of what might have prompted the need for sanctuary. Perhaps we can find a way forward by considering how such a prayer would have functioned in ancient Israel's cult. The comments of Erhard Gerstenberger provide general assistance.[34] He argues that sociological studies suggest that ancient Near Eastern cultures used rituals for daily needs within small, primary social groups. Prayers from such rituals were later linked to social institutions such as state and monarchy, but the prayers still carried import for individuals. So small group rituals were taken over by the royal cult rather than a primary royal cult being democratized. These small group rituals would have been presided over by an officiant, a ritual specialist. The specialist would have had some flexibility, given the nature of the crisis, and perhaps some connection with sanctuaries. In line with the comments of Gerstenberger and others, the asylum is not one of residence in the temple. Rather, the text reflects a kind of variant of the rite of asylum. The cultic official (priest?), likely in the temple court in this case, intervenes in the crisis and offers the word from God that the speaker is to continue under God's protection.[35]

Such a cultic word would have carried great force in that community. Ronald E. Clements indicates the significance of the cultic decision.[36] He examines those passages, especially in the Psalms, which speak of dwelling in the temple forever. He argues that such language, as in Ps. 61:5, refers to going to the temple to worship. The same language is used that

---

[34]Gerstenberger, *Psalms*, 7, 9, 14. See also idem, *Der Bittende Mensch: Bittritual und Klagelied des Einzelnen im Alten Testament*, WMANT 51 (Neukirchen-Vluyn: Neukirchener Verlag, 1980); Rainer Albertz, *Persönliche Frömmigkeit und offizielle Religion*, CThM 9 (Stuttgart: Calwer Verlag, 1978).

[35]See Gerstenberger, *Psalms*, 7, 9, 14, 157; Milgrom, "Sancta Contagion," 306; H. C. Thompson, "The Right of Entry to the Temple in the Old Testament," *TGUOS* 21 (1965–1966): 25-34. The psalm reflects a longing for the protection of the divine presence centered in the Temple. Such a yearning does not necessarily indicate geographical distance from Jerusalem; Keel's interpretation of מִקְצֵה הָאָרֶץ would appear to be sound. Indeed, the brevity and movement of the psalm, along with its Temple imagery, support the view that the psalm was used in Jerusalem.

[36]Ronald E. Clements, "Temple and Land: A Significant Aspect of Israel's Worship," *TGUOS* 19 (1963): 16-28.

way in the Psalter's Entrance Liturgies (Pss. 15; 24), and such an interpretation fits the parallelism of Ps. 27:4. Clements further argues—and
this is the prime point of his essay—that the privilege of worshiping
carried with it the further privilege of dwelling on God's land, of being
a sojourner רֵג in the promised land (Lev. 25:23; Ps. 39:13). Three arguments support this last contention:

(1) The temple mount is understood as the dwelling place of God.
The mountain represents the earth with its powers of life and fertility before God from whom blessing flows to the land by way of the mountain.
The sanctuary then represents land, primarily the worshiper's land, before
God. Possession of Mount Zion as God's abode is closely connected with
the right to dwell on the land (see Exod. 15:13-17; Ps. 78:54; Isa. 11:9;
57:13). So the temple mount represents the land before God. Worshiping
there has to do with maintaining responsibilities toward the land's owner
and Lord, who holds the power to distribute land. Clements suggests a
Jebusite background for this view and that Mount Zion was representative
of the land. Worshiping on God's holy hill carried the privilege of dwelling on the land which it symbolized.

(2) The temple is a symbol of the land; and it is also a symbol of the
world, of the universe where God dwells. Cosmic symbolism was a part
of the temple precincts: the bronze sea and especially the spring, the
water bringing renewal and fertility to the creation. This water brings
blessing to people and land and is available to all who worship in the
temple, not just cultic personnel. Such blessings relate to daily necessi-
ties, which carry spiritual and holy significance. The availability of
blessing is tied to loyalty to God. The unworthy may not worship in the
temple (Pss. 5:5; 24:1, 3), for loyalty to God expressed in worship carries
with it the blessing of dwelling on God's land. See Ps. 37:3, 9, 11, 18-19,
27, 29, 34, and Pss. 36:9-10; 46:5; 65:5; 92:13-15; Joel 4:18; Isa. 33:21;
Zech. 14:8; Ezek. 47:1ff.; Exod. 34:24.

(3) The purpose of the cult was to actualize divine activity on earth,
divine blessing and fertility for land and people, and avoidance of
trouble. God's goodness and mercy are to be extended to all in every
area of life. It was thus important to worship, especially at the festivals,
so one could continue on the land. Cultic officials writing the Psalms saw
this teaching as an important one; the future of the people depended on
it. So to dwell (worship) in the temple carried with it the privilege of

dwelling on the land.[37] Thus our psalm's reference to dwelling in God's tent forever (v. 5) holds a great deal of significance. In line with the work of Clements, divine intervention gave the speaker official status as a member of the community of ancient Israel with the concomitant blessings including land ownership (יִרְשׁוּ in v. 6). So the favorable response to the prayer carried life importance beyond the current set of circumstances.[38]

Further, it is the king who is guarantor of such a practice and its justice in that society—thus, the prayer for the king.[39] As we have seen, it is possible that the speaker of the prayer for protection is the king who seeks protection in the face of (military?) enemies. The protection would be in line with the special relationship between God and king. The question hinges on whether it is more natural to read the whole psalm as words of the king who refers to himself in the third person in vv. 7-8 or as the words of a petitioner who then prays for the king as an extension of the setting.[40] I would have expected something like "your servant David" if the king were speaking rather than simply מֶלֶךְ.[41] Thus I do

---

[37]See Eryl W. Davies, "Land: Its Rights and Privileges," *The World of Ancient Israel*, ed. Ronald E. Clements (Cambridge: Cambridge University Press, 1989) 349-69, for further comments on the significance of land.

[38]If the interpreter translates the psalm as a prayer of confidence rather than petition, the setting for the whole psalm would be after the protection has been granted.

[39]The prayer for the king (vv. 7-8) and connections with the temple clearly indicate that the psalm as a whole dates from the time of the Davidic monarchy and temple, even if vv. 7-8 are an editorial addition.

[40]Attempts, including ours, to account for the presence of an intercession for the king in a nonroyal psalm often focus on solidarity between king and people as well as the understanding of the king as a channel of divine blessing for the community. See, in addition to previous references, Carroll Stuhlmueller, *Psalms 1 (Psalms 1-72)*, OTM (Wilmington DE: Michael Glazier, 1983) 280-81; Oesterley, *Psalms*, 301; J. W. Rogerson and J. W. McKay, *Psalms 51-100*, CBC (Cambridge: University Press, 1977) 59; Anderson, *Psalms*, 1:446-47.

[41]Royal Psalms use the more personal terminology. See Pss. 2, 18, 20, 21, 45, 72, 89, 110, 132, and 144, and contrast Pss. 61 and 63, which I take not to be royal compositions. The Royal Psalms that do use מֶלֶךְ also employ other royal titles.

not think the speaker was the king, but certainty on the subject is not possible.[42]

Our proposal of a setting for Psalm 61 accounts for the psalm's nature as a prayer for protection, for the connections with temple and king, and for the "heritage" in v. 6. However, the proposal is necessarily a construction; it can only be tentative. The psalm does not fill in the gaps of setting for us. The text does not give an explicit description of the crisis at hand. The whole process of constructing a setting for the psalm does remind us, however, that the poem was not a free-floating piece of literature. It was a part of ancient Israel's cult and life. It is not an abstraction but a prayer very much out of the depths of the experience of ancient Israel.

Thus far, our discussion has accounted for the cultic background, both general and specific, of Psalm 61. What about the psalm's ancient Israelite social matrix? Gerstenberger's comments are relevant here, as is the work of Norman Gottwald.[43]

> Nonetheless, insofar as the royal ideology asserted social justice as its obligation, priests had some elbowroom to ameliorate the worst abuses by giving cultic support to the wronged even when the courts failed and by helping to build and disseminate a community climate for the defense of traditional rights. Because the socially powerful had a big stake in the cult, it is likely that they contested priestly sympathy for their victims but could not totally repress accepted cultic procedures. This may be one reason for the vagueness of language in the laments, since to have been more explicit might have brought further recriminations and penalties on the worshipers and priests alike.[44]

The social matrix from which Psalm 61 derives is the Jerusalem royal/cultic institutions. No text comes from a disinterested social matrix.

---

[42]Kraus, Gunkel, Dahood, and other commentators have noted similar intrusive royal prayers from the ancient Near East. Such prayers would fit a cult supported by the monarchy. On balance, however, such parallels provide little help in resolving the issue; the identity of the speaker is not unambiguous in those cases either. See Johnson, *The Cultic Prophet,* 353.

[43]Norman K. Gottwald, *The Hebrew Bible: A Socioliterary Introduction* (Philadelphia: Fortress Press, 1985) 527-28, 537-41.

[44]Ibid., 540.

In one sense, the text supports the established position of the royal/cultic institutions; but it does so in defense of justice in the midst of social tensions which ancient Israel experienced, to judge from much of the Old Testament, as do other societies.[45]

Intent

The psalm is a prayer for protection and inclusion in the ancient Israelite community. Form critics continue the discussion by asking about the intent of the text. The psalm provides a prayer for protection and encourages the community to seek protection in the God who hears and acts for the wronged among the faithful. The prayer also addresses God and, in confidence, seeks God's help.

Conclusion

Our discussion of the background of Psalm 61 has suggested that it is a petition for protection associated with the sanctuary, a petition for God to snatch the speaker from the power of death and oppression to the hope of life and justice. The cult supports that cry. What became of Psalm 61 when there was no more cult? How did it become a part of our book of Psalms? The investigation continues in the next chapter.[46]

---

[45]An alternative, more suspicious reading of the text would suggest that the priests would use their position to further oppression. Our view, however, seems more in sympathy with the text. For a "suspicious" reading of the hymns of the Psalter, see Walter Brueggemann, *Israel's Praise*.

[46]The next chapter will show that a text (genre) can be used in more than one setting. See B. O. Long, "Recent Field Studies in Oral Literature and the Question of *Sitz im Leben*," *Semeia* 5 (1976): 35-49; idem, "Recent Field Studies in Oral Literature and Their Bearing on Old Testament Criticism," *VT* 26 (1976): 187-98; Tate, *Psalms 51-100*, 109-16.

Canon

Introduction

When Psalm 61 invites the reader to ask about the references to God's tent and wings, the vows, and the king, the answers come from a cultic setting. But another question arises. What happened to the psalm after the monarchy, the temple, and its cult were destroyed? What happened to the psalm after its origin? How did it come to be included in our Psalter? To ignore such questions would have us lock our psalm in an ancient past. The text, and our hermeneutic of curiosity, invites us forward, as well as backward. What was its continuing life from its origin until its inclusion in the canon? How did the early Jewish community appropriate the text? How did it understand the originally cultic references, and what about the king?

Psalm 61 invites us to ask these questions. They have also been asked by a number of contemporary Old Testament scholars. Brevard Childs has led the way in developing a new approach for reading the Bible, a canonical approach which centers on the questions in the preceding paragraph.[1] Childs argues that the historical-critical approach has left the canon locked in the past and left the Bible inaccessible for the contemporary community of faith. Scholars have concentrated too much on

---

[1]See esp. B. S. Childs, *Biblical Theology in Crisis* (Philadelphia: Westminster Press, 1970); *The Book of Exodus*, OTL (Philadelphia: Westminster Press, 1974); *Introduction to the Old Testament as Scripture* (Philadelphia: Fortress Press, 1979); "The Exegetical Significance of Canon for the Study of the Old Testament," *Congress Volume, Göttingen 1977*, VTSup 29 (Leiden: E. J. Brill, 1978) 66-80; *Old Testament Theology in a Canonical Context* (Philadelphia: Fortress Press, 1985); *The New Testament as Canon: An Introduction* (Philadelphia: Fortress Press, 1984); and *Biblical Theology of the Old and New Testaments* (Minneapolis: Augsburg/Fortress Press, 1993).

the prehistory of biblical texts, how they originated, rather than on their canonical form. The way out of such a failure on the part of biblical scholars begins with recognizing the full significance of the Old Testament as canon, as the authoritative Scripture we now have. Thus Childs concentrates on the final form of the Bible, its canonical shape.

Childs's work has occasioned a great deal of debate.[2] There has been much discussion of his understanding of canon and whether it is appropriate, of the relationship between Childs's approach and the historical-critical approach, of the relationship between Childs's approach and theology, and of the relationship between Childs's approach and recent literary-critical theory, as well as other issues.[3] Some have followed Childs;

---

[2]Of particular significance is *JSOT* 16 (1980). The issue is devoted to Childs's Old Testament introduction: Bonnie Kittel, "Brevard Childs's Development of the Canonical Approach," 2-11; James Barr, "Childs's Introduction to the Old Testament as Scripture," 12-23; J. Blenkinsopp, "A New Kind of Introduction: Professor Childs's *Introduction to the Old Testament as Scripture*," 24-27; H. Cazelles, "The Canonical Approach to Torah and Prophets," 28-31; George M. Landes, "The Canonical Approach to Introducing the Old Testament: Prodigy and Problems," 32-39; R. E. Murphy, "The Old Testament as Scripture," 40-44; Rudolf Smend, "Questions About the Importance of the Canon in an Old Testament Introduction," 45-51; Brevard S. Childs, "Response to Reviewers of *Introduction to the OT as Scripture*," 52-60. Another set of such responses is in *HBT* 2 (1980): Bruce C. Birch, "Tradition, Canon and Biblical Theology," 113-25; Douglas A. Knight, "Canon and the History of Tradition: A Critique of Brevard S. Childs's *Introduction to the Old Testament as Scripture*," 127-49; James L. Mays, "What Is Written: A Response to Brevard Childs's *Introduction to the Old Testament as Scripture*," 151-63; David P. Polk, "Brevard Childs's *Introduction to the Old Testament as Scripture*," 165-71; James A. Sanders, "Canonical Context and Canonical Criticism," 173-97; Brevard S. Childs, "A Response," 199-211. See also Gerald T. Sheppard, "Canon Criticism: The Proposal of Brevard Childs and an Assessment for Evangelical Hermeneutics," *Studia Biblica et Theologica* 4 (1974): 3-17; Mikeal C. Parsons, "Canonical Criticism," in *New Testament Criticism and Interpretation*, ed. David Black and David Dockery (Grand Rapids: Zondervan, 1991) 255-94.

[3]See Barton, *Reading the Old Testament*, esp. 77-103. Barton's critique is sympathetic, yet penetrating.

others have rejected his work out of hand.[4] A number of scholars have voiced appreciation for the issues Childs has raised but have suggested different ways to deal with them. This latter approach is the path I wish to pursue.

First, however, we need to say a word about the work of James Sanders. Sanders is the other main proponent of canonical criticism, but he does things rather differently than does Childs.[5] While Childs concentrates on the final, canonical shape for the text, Sanders understands canon more in terms of a process. His work has links with tradition history; he is interested in how a text gathers up past traditions or themes from ancient Israel's faith and makes use of them in its own setting. So hermeneutics and then theology become important for Sanders. The hermeneutics used in developing the canonical form of the text provide clues for contemporary interpreters in the task of appropriating the text today.[6] Sanders's work is not as specific as Childs's and has not brought as much debate. Nonetheless, it is worth noting.

This chapter proposes to relate "canon criticism" to Psalm 61. What do I mean by the term? The simple definition would be the serious, historical analysis of canon, in this case Psalm 61 as part of a canon.[7] The

---

[4]For the most pungent criticism of Childs's work, see James Barr, *Holy Scripture: Canon, Authority, Criticism* (Oxford: Clarendon Press, 1983). Also see Sean E. McEvenue, "The Old Testament, Scripture or Theology?" *Int* 35 (1981): 229-42.

[5]See James A. Sanders, *Torah and Canon* (Philadelphia: Fortress Press, 1972); *Canon and Community: A Guide to Canonical Criticism*, GBS (Philadelphia: Fortress Press, 1984); "Adaptable for Life: The Nature and Function of Canon," in *Magnalia Dei: The Mighty Acts of God* (Garden City NY: Doubleday, 1976) 531-60; "Biblical Criticism and the Bible as Canon," *USQR* 32 (1977): 157-65; and *From Sacred Story to Sacred Text: Canon as Paradigm* (Philadelphia: Fortress Press, 1987). Also worthy of note is Childs's review of *Torah and Canon* in *Interpretation* 27 (1973): 88-91.

[6]Sanders's concerns with hermeneutics and theology are especially evident in *Canon and Community*. Take note of his hermeneutical triangle on p. 77. Such issues necessarily bring subjectivity into the debate.

[7]The question of which canon is a particularly vexed one. For our purposes, we will be using the Protestant Old Testament canon, based on the Hebrew canon. That decision has a confessional and scholarly basis; the Hebrew canon

term seems more apt, in analogy with other types of criticism, than San-ders's "canonical criticism"; Childs has eschewed both terms. He prefers the "canonical approach" or "exegesis in a canonical context," because he envisions the approach as replacing that of historical criticism. At that point, I differ from Childs considerably. I have been arguing for a herme-neutical pluralism which includes traditional forms of historical criticism and newer methodologies. Questions about Psalm 61 in its canonical con-text are significant and need to be asked, but we have already seen that the questions of text and form criticism also provide the psalm's interpre-ters with valuable information.

In what follows, canon criticism will be in dialogue with Psalm 61 in three ways. First, we will deal with the traditional concerns of redac-tion criticism.[8] How did Psalm 61 come to its final, canonical form? Second, what can we say, in line with Childs, about the canonical shape of Psalm 61? What are the contours of the text in its canonical context? Third, how does the psalm relate to the rest of the canon, especially other traditions formative for the canon?

The purpose so far in this chapter has not been to enter the debate over canon criticism in any significant way, but simply to clarify my understanding of the procedures to be used with Psalm 61.[9] To such we now move; what is the shape of a canonical reading of the text?

Redaction

Did Psalm 61 undergo redaction? We have already seen that a num-ber of commentators suggest that vv. 7-8, the prayer for the king, form

---

is the one primarily used in Old Testament scholarship. One could operate on the basis of the Alexandrian canon; or one could, in a Christian context, include the New Testament.

[8]Redaction criticism deals with the redaction or editing of texts. On the method, see Barton, *Reading the Old Testament*, esp. 45-60. For examples, see Martin Noth, *The Deuteronomistic History*, JSOTSup 15 (Sheffield: JSOT, 1981); R. E. Clements, "Patterns in the Prophetic Canon," *Canon and Authority*, ed. G. W. Coats and B. O. Long (Philadelphia: Westminster Press, 1977): 42-55.

[9]See McCann, *Shape and Shaping of the Psalter*; idem, *Theological Introduc-tion to the Book of Psalms*; and *Int* 46/2 (1992).

an editorial addition.[10] This view is not without basis. Verses 1-6, 9 read like many other individual laments and, if one is accustomed to such texts, the prayer for the king in vv. 7-8 seems like a sudden intrusion. Thus one can see how an interpreter would suggest that the intercession for the king is an editorial addition. However, such a criterion depends too heavily on our own desire for consistency. In addition, our analysis of the form of the psalm suggests that vv. 7-9 belong together as a verse paragraph set off with the inclusio יָמִים עַל־יְמֵי, "days upon days," and יוֹם יוֹם, "day by day." We also noted connections between this last section of the psalm and other parts in vv. 1-6. Verse 9 exhibits some parallels to v. 6 with נְדָרַי, "my vows," and שְׁמֶךָ, "your name." Verse 8 also speaks of protection for the king as v. 5 does for the speaker. Note also the use of עוֹלָם in v. 8 and עוֹלָמִים in v. 5 as well as לִפְנֵי in v. 8 and מִפְּנֵי in v. 4. We also accounted, in the last chapter, for the whole of Psalm 61 with one setting. Thus it seems unlikely that vv. 7-8 are an editorial addition to the psalm. The poem seems to have originated as a piece.

However, if vv. 7-8 were an addition to the text, they would serve the function of broadening the reference of the prayer beyond an individual to the community. The king was to be the channel of blessing for the whole of ancient Israel. Thus the redactor in this prayer would be seeking, through that channel, God's favorable hearing and action for the whole community, just as it had been experienced by the individual speaking the prayer (v. 6). The final form of the text would then apply to both individual and community.

Canonical Shape

If traditional redaction of Psalm 61 is unlikely, a more profitable approach might be found in Childs's "canonical shape" of the text.[11] Childs speaks of the canonical shape of the Psalter; what can we say about Psalm 61 within that context? What are the contours of the text as

---

[10]E.g., Gunkel, *Psalmen*, 26-261; Taylor and McCullough, "The Book of the Psalms," 318. Kraus, *Psalms 60-150*, 8-10, and Schmidt, *Psalmen*, 116, treat the verses separately.

[11]See Childs, *Old Testament as Scripture*, 504-25, for his treatment of the Psalter.

we find it in its final form, in its canonical context? We might call this approach "composition criticism"; it deals with the factors operative in the composition and placement of the text as we have it in the canon. It is a more holistic approach. The question also has contacts with San-ders's attempts to determine the hermeneutics at work in the composition of a canonical text.[12] Discovering such hermeneutics is difficult, but when we read Psalm 61 in its canonical context rather than in its original con-text, certain elements in the shape of the text come to the fore.

How did our text reach its canonical shape? The psalm was com-posed during the time of the Davidic monarchy in Jerusalem. The com-poser(s) are most likely to be found among the temple personnel.[13] The text would have been used on appropriate occasions as part of worship there.[14] The poem is among the Davidic collection of Psalms, a collection dominated by individual laments, and is linked with similar texts as we shall see. In the postexilic period when the theological/worship leaders of early Judaism continued to put the canonical Psalter together, they in-cluded our text as Psalm 61.[15] Various concerns were operative in the compilation of the Psalter, concerns which indicate that the community shaped this collection of Psalms to meet its needs in worship and life.[16] Our treatment of the canonical shape of Psalm 61 will reflect some of the ways the community shaped the Psalter so they could continue to use it

---

[12]See Sanders, *Canon and Community*.

[13]See Mowinckel, *Psalms in Israel's Worship*, 2:85ff.

[14]In line with our description and the telling views of Mowinckel, *Psalms in Israel's Worship*, 1:1-41, we thus refer to the speaker/singer of the text, or wor-shiper(s), rather than the psalmist, the composer.

[15]On the compilation of the Psalter, see Claus Westermann, *Praise and La-ment in the Psalms* (Atlanta: John Knox Press, 1981) 250-58; Patrick D. Miller, Jr., *Interpreting the Psalms* (Philadelphia: Fortress Press, 1986) 11-15; Gerald H. Wilson, *The Editing of the Hebrew Psalter*, SBLDS 76 (Chico CA: Scholars Press, 1985); idem, "The Qumran Psalms Manuscripts and the Consecutive Arrangement of Psalms in the Hebrew Psalter," *CBQ* 45 (1983): 377-88; idem, "Evidence of Editorial Divisions in the Hebrew Psalter," *VT* 34 (1984): 337-52; idem, "The Use of Royal Psalms at the 'Seams' of the Hebrew Psalter," *JSOT* 35 (1986): 85-94; and Bellinger, *Psalms*, 6-12. Our text was also included in the Elohistic Psalter.

[16]See Bellinger, *Psalms*, 27-32.

in their life and worship. When we read Psalm 61 in its canonical context, certain of these features in the text come to the fore. What are they?[17]

Community Emphasis. We have already noted that vv. 7-8 voice intercession for the king.[18] The prayer for the king reflects the background that the king is to be the channel of God's blessing for the whole community, including the speaker of Psalm 61. The king's continual rule before God (v. 8) indicates that the king is just and righteous, and thus the community will experience the fruits of such faithfulness in God's blessing. God grants the speaker a favorable hearing. The prayer for the king implies the hope that such will also be true for the community.

Influence from the Exile. The Babylonian exile was a traumatic experience for ancient Israel, and Becker has suggested the community reinterpreted psalms in light of that experience.[19] Such may well have been the case with Psalm 61. We have interpreted the phrase מִקְצֵה הָאָרֶץ, "from the end of the earth," in terms of Sheol rather than in terms of geography. However, for the community in exile, Babylon must have seemed the end of the earth and the edge of Death. They may well have reinterpreted Psalm 61 in light of that setting. The community prayed for protection in an uncertain time. Two other features of the text would have enabled the exilic community to draw strength from our psalm. The "heritage" (יְרֻשַּׁת) of v. 6 in reference to the land might provide hope for returning to the land. Also of significance is the reference to the king. The exilic community may well have hoped for the restoration of monarchy. In these ways the psalm could be appropriated by the community in

---

[17]Thus while our method in this chapter has taken many of its cues from Childs, we execute the operation rather differently. My method is a kind of redaction criticism centering on the redaction of the psalm and the compilation of the Psalter. Particularly relevant is how the community reread or reinterpreted the psalm. How did they view it after there was no cult? All such questions are relevant to reading Ps. 61 in its canonical context. See Barton, *Reading the Old Testament*, 101-103, esp. n. 12, and Childs, "Exegetical Significance," 68-69.

[18]On the significance of the king for ancient Israel, see Bellinger, *Psalms*, 106-23.

[19]Joachim Becker, *Israel Deutet seine Psalmen: Urformen und Neuinterpretation in den Psalmen*, SBS 18 (Stuttgart: Katholisches Bibelwerk, 1966); see Childs, *Old Testament as Scripture*, 517-20.

exile, and thus the text is included in the Psalter which continued to feed ancient Israel's life from the time of the monarchy through the exile.

Hope for the Future. The reinterpretation of the psalm in light of the exile emphasizes hope for the future. The hope for the king and for God's protection in the future are notable in this psalm and could be applied at any juncture of the community's story. Childs has suggested that the canonical shape of the Psalter includes an eschatological hope and a messianic view of the Royal Psalms.[20] Ps. 61:7-8 certainly initially referred to the Davidic king and dynasty in Jerusalem, but by the time of the compilation of the Psalter, there was no king in Jerusalem. The community had come to understand such references to the king as messianic ones bearing witness to hope for the messianic kingdom.[21] The canonical Psalm 61 would have provided significant hope for the future for the early Jewish community.

The Language of the Psalter. We have already had occasion to note the ambiguity in the language of Psalm 61. The language of the Psalter is general, even vague, in nature.

> Such language is part of the reason the Psalms have remained so significant through the centuries. The language is universally applicable and usable. It is adaptable for life and open to use by many. This feature is also part of ancient Israel's reinterpretation of these texts. This kind of language makes possible the application of these texts to a community no longer tied to the preexilic Jerusalem cult. Clues of original cultic settings are still present, but the language is also now open to a broader interpretation as Scripture for the life of faith.[22]

The language of Psalm 61 is no less capable of such a "universalizing" interpretation. Any petitioner in a difficult crisis could, with this psalm, pray for God's protection. While the references in v. 4 בְּאָהָלְךָ,

---

[20]Childs, *Old Testament as Scripture*, 515-18.

[21]See Tate, *Psalms 51-100*, 109-16.

[22]Bellinger, *Psalms*, 29. See also Bellinger, *Psalmody and Prophecy*, 24-27; Miller, *Interpreting the Psalms*, 11-13; Sanders, "Nature and Function," 531-60. Note Sanders's decription of canon as stable and yet adaptable language which is life-giving. The general nature of the language of psalms is one of the reasons determining a setting for the psalm is difficult. However, the psalmic language also enables the text to have continuing applicability beyond its original setting.

"in your tent," and בְּסֵתֶר כְּנָפֶיךָ, "in the shelter of your wings," no doubt initially referred to the temple, they could certainly be interpreted in a more metaphorical, broadly spiritual way after the destruction of the temple.[23] The same is true of the psalm's other cultic references. Even the reference to the king (vv. 7-8) is sufficiently general to be applicable to a foreign ruler over the Jewish people after the fall of Jerusalem. The use of אֱלֹהִים, "God," a more generic term than "Yahweh," may also reflect a wider cultural setting. So the language of our psalm is typical and general to enable its universal applicability.

Superscription. The superscription is part of the community's reinterpretation of the text.[24] This psalm's superscription includes the liturgical collection from which the psalm derived and technical terms related to use in worship. The psalm has reached its canonical placement by way of a process and has its home in worship, a specific event that was central to the faith community and an event which has continued through the ages for that community. The association of the psalm with David is characteristic of many psalms. Elsewhere in the superscriptions to psalms, David is pictured not as glorious king but as representative person engaged in the life of faith. Readers of these psalms can again see the texts' relevance to their own pilgrimage of faith.[25]

The Organization of the Psalter. The Psalter was shaped over time as a collection for the life of faith. The shaping included redacting specific psalms as well as putting the poems in sequence. The introductory psalm makes it clear that the book is to be read as instruction ("torah" in Ps. 1:2) for righteous living. The book then concentrates on an essential aspect of such living—prayer. Individual laments dominate the first part

---

[23]The phrases in question could also have carried the metaphorical meaning at the same time they referred to the temple. The nature of psalmic language—whether it is literal, metaphorical, mythological or some combination thereof—is not easy to determine. E.g., Ps. 6 is probably a prayer of one who is sick; see esp. vv. 3, 8. However, Jeremiah used the same language to describe his difficulty in accomplishing his prophetic task; see Jer. 15:15-21; 17:12-18.

[24]See Bellinger, *Psalms*, 8-12, 29.

[25]Particularly helpful on the psalm superscriptions are B. S. Childs, "Psalm Titles and Midrashic Exegesis," *JSS* 16 (1971): 137-50, and John F. A. Sawyer, "An Analysis of the Context and Meaning of the Psalm-Headings," *TGUOS* 22 (1967–1968): 26-38.

of the book, while community praise comes to the fore in the latter parts. The collection's concluding psalm calls for exuberant praise indicating the satisfaction found in righteous living. The compilation of the Psalms then also reflects the process of redaction and reinterpetation. The configuration of the canonical shape of the book provides a context for interpretation.

Psalm 61 is among the Davidic psalms in the first two books, dominated by individual laments. It looks forward to community praise. The compilation of the Psalter was tied to the representative pilgrimage of faith. That canonical context is important for interpretation.[26]

Psalm 61. Up to this point, the analysis has attended to a broader canonical context (the Psalter). Can I be more specific about the placement of Psalm 61? The psalm is surrounded by laments (Pss. 51-64). Psalm 60 reflects a battle context, perhaps away from Jerusalem. That may have provided a connection to the beginning of Psalm 61 ("from the end of the earth"). The laments leading up to our psalm speak often of enemies. That may be important since Psalm 61 only mentions the enemy once (v. 4), but the laments following Psalm 61 seem to give a more significant place to trust. In its immediate context, our psalm reflects something of a shift. The remainder of the second book is more hopeful.

Psalm 61 has specific connections with Psalm 62 (see vv. 3, 7-8) and Psalm 63 (see vv. 3, 5, 8, 12). God as fortress and refuge is central to these connections. Note especially the reference to the protection of God's "wings" in Psalm 63:8. Psalms 60-63 all reflect a yearning for the sanctuary God provides. Even this brief analysis has revealed connections that imply intentionality in the canonical placement of Psalm 61.

The canonical context of Psalm 61, then, provides the interpreter with helpful information. The psalm's canonical placement is significant. The community interpreted the psalm as looking to the future with hope and confidence. Thus the psalm could continue to function as a source of faith and identity.

---

[26]Walter Brueggemann, "Bounded by Obedience and Praise: The Psalms as Canon," *JSOT* 50 (1991): 63-92.

Tradition History

The full canonical context of Psalm 61 goes beyond the Psalter, of course, to the whole Old Testament and beyond that. The psalms' confident dialogue of faith brings to mind much which is central to Old Testament theology. What are the particular thematic connections between Psalm 61 and other Old Testament texts? Our question has connections with the history-of-traditions method of interpretation, which traces the history of traditions or themes through the Old Testament.[27] Psalm 61 applies traditions in its own way as part of that history. Three traditional connections are significant.

1. The "tent" traditions. Verse 5 refers to God's tent (אֹהֶל). Such a reference reminds us of the traditions elsewhere about God's tent or sanctuary, especially in Exodus and Leviticus and in the move toward a temple in Jerusalem. The tent was a place of gathering to encounter God in worship and to receive guidance. It becomes the primary symbol of God's presence with the faith community ancient Israel.[28] In Psalm 61, the tent is primarily a place of protection, a holy place because of God's protecting presence.

2. The "name" traditions. Verse 6 speaks of "those who fear your name" (יִרְאֵי שְׁמֶךָ) and v. 9 of "your name" (שִׁמְךָ). Such references,

---

[27]On the method, see Walter E. Rast, *Tradition History and the Old Testament*, GBS (Philadelphia: Fortress Press, 1972). Significant examples of the use of the method include Martin Noth, *A History of Pentateuchal Traditions*, trans. Bernhard W. Anderson (Engelwood Cliffs NJ: Prentice-Hall, 1972); E. W. Nicholson, *Deuteronomy and Tradition* (Philadelphia: Fortress Press, 1967); Beyerlin, *Weisheitlich-kultische Heilsordnung*; idem, *"Wir sind wie Traeumende:" Studien zum 126. Psalm*, SBS 89 (Stuttgart: Verlag Katholisches Bibelwerk, 1978); and idem, *Weisheitliche Vergewisserung mit Bezug auf den Zionskult: Studien zum 125. Psalm*, OBO 68 (Göttingen: Vandenhoeck & Ruprecht, 1985).

[28]See, e.g., R. E. Clements, *God and Temple: The Presence of God in Israel's Worship* (Philadelphia: Fortress, 1965); idem, *Exodus*, CBC (Cambridge: Cambridge University Press, 1972); Menaham Haran, *Temples and Temple-Service in Ancient Israel: An Inquiry into the Character of Cult Phenomena and the Historical Setting of the Priestly School* (Oxford: Clarendon Press, 1978); and bibliography reflected in Walter Brueggemann and Hans Walter Wolff, *The Vitality of Old Testament Traditions*, 2nd ed. (Atlanta: John Knox Press, 1982).

especially the phrase in v. 6, are quite reminiscent of the Deuteronomic "name" theology.[29] The Deuteronomic use of יְרֻשָּׁה, "heritage," is also relevant. שֵׁם was a circumlocution for God. The "place where God would choose to make the divine *name* to dwell there" was the temple; God could thus be present there but not limited to that locale. Those fearing God's name are those faithful to the covenant with God. They are the ones who encounter covenant blessing. In Psalm 61, the speaker has been declared among the covenant faithful and thus the community of faith and worship. The petitioner enjoys the privileges of sojourning under the aegis of God's presence and looking to the future with hope.

3. The Davidic traditions. Verses 7-8 certainly reflect the royal Davidic traditions in the Hebrew canon.[30] Of particular importance is the Davidic covenant promise given by Nathan in 2 Samuel 7, but other royal traditions also come into play. The promise was that David and his sons would rule over the people in Jerusalem. We have already seen that the king was to be a channel of blessing for the people. The prayer in Psalm 61 is that the king and dynasty have a long life and the protection of חֶסֶד וֶאֱמֶת. Such divine protection would indicate that the king has been just and will thus ensure blessing for the people. The king would be the guarantor of the speaker's safety.[31]

These traditions come together in Psalm 61 in the context of divine protection for the petitioner. King and temple become significant actualities toward that end, a blessing for those who fear God's name. The psalm echoes the richness of Old Testament traditions and shows one way those traditions are put to use. Such a canonical reading of our text shows the continuing relationship between ancient Israel and God, and it helps clarify the focus of the prayer.

---

[29]See Hans Bietenhard, ὄνομα, ὀνομάζω, ἐπονομάζω, ψευδώνυμος, *TDNT* 5:256; Gerhard von Rad, *Studies in Deuteronomy*, SBT 9 (London: SCM Press, 1953) esp. 37-44.

[30]See, e.g., Gerhard von Rad, *Old Testament Theology*, vol. 1, trans. D. M. G. Stalker (New York: Harper & Row, 1962) 306-54; R. E. Clements, *Abraham and David: Genesis 15 and Its Meaning for Israelite Tradition*, SBT 2nd ser. 5 (London: SCM Press, 1967); David Gunn, *The Story of King David: Genre and Interpretation*, JSOTSup 6 (Sheffield: JSOT Press, 1978).

[31]If the speaker is the king, the prayer would be to bring the promises of the Davidic tradition to fulfillment.

Conclusion

This chapter has sought to read Psalm 61 in its canonical context.[32] The prayer originated as a piece and is now in the context of the Psalter with similar psalms. The psalm's canonical shape enabled the faith community to appropriate the prayer after the demise of the Temple cult; the prayer looks to the future with hope in the God who protects. The community of synagogue and local sanctuaries became a focal point for that protection. The psalm has contacts with other Old Testament traditions as it prays for help. So a canonical approach to Psalm 61 produces a reading of a prayer which seeks God's protection in the broadest sense, in whatever crisis the speaker experiences; and the community is central to this concern.

This chapter concludes the parts of our study which have a predominantly historical emphasis. We have explored the text, form, setting, and final form of Psalm 61. What if we began the interpretive task not with questions about how the text developed, but with questions about the literary phenomenon of the text before us now? This chapter on canon moves us in that direction. Let us push forward to the text as an artifact of language.

---

[32]In recent years, the Book of Psalms Group of the Society of Biblical Literature has with significant profit explored the shape and shaping of the Psalter. Such studies are in their infancy, but we can expect further contributions in this area in the near future. A canonical approach also hints at the issue of reception history. How have communities read the Psalter—and Psalm 61? Liturgical uses of the psalm would be important. Such an investigation is beyond the scope of our study but could provide the interpreter with significant information. See Wilson, "The Use of Royal Psalms," 85-88.

Rhetoric

Introduction

Our discussions oriented toward historical issues have brought us back to our starting point: the extant text of Psalm 61. The hermeneutical model described in the introduction spoke of writer, text, and reader as part of the interpretive process. The preceding chapters give primacy to matters surrounding the psalm's writer, or at least its origin and development. This chapter approaches Psalm 61 from the point of view of "the text itself." Of particular importance are the ways the text uses language to create and communicate its message so as to convince its reader. The interpreter seeks to discover the way the text uses language by way of a careful reading. Such a task is surely central to interpretation.

The text invites the reader to take such an approach. As poetry the psalm seeks to draw in the reader. The careful reader will then begin to see the strategies the text uses in order to gain and hold the reader's attention. Such reading necessitates questions we have already noted: What is the movement of the psalm? How do its parts relate? (See chap. 2, above.) What kind of poetic devices does it use? What kind of function does the text serve in the receiving community? Of what does it seek to persuade? What is the text about, at its most basic level; why is the text in the canon? Any text invites such questions.

Old Testament scholarship using such an approach has generally gone under the rubric of rhetorical criticism. We noted the use of such a method in chapter 2 ("Form"); the term and its program seem to have derived from James Muilenburg.[1] Definition of the term has been a slippery

---

[1] See nn. 41 and 42 in chap. 1. On the method and its development, see *Rhetorical Criticism: Essays in Honor of James Muilenburg*, ed. Jared J. Jackson and Martin Kessler, PTMS 1 (Pittsburgh: Pickwick Press, 1974) which presents examples of rhetorical criticism.

job, but most of the work done in the area has concentrated on what might be called poetic style.[2] Central is the identification of rhetorical or stylistic devices. Such an approach has gained popularity in contemporary Old Testament scholarship.[3] It concentrates on the extant form of the text rather than on questions of sociohistorical, or cultural, background.

The method bears clear and explicit influence from the movement in literary criticism called the New Criticism.[4] This movement reacted against a biographical criticism which interpreted texts in light of external factors present in the life of the author. We have already seen the importance of the "intentional fallacy" as described by the New Critics. Literary critics have now moved on from the New Criticism,[5] but its influence is still being felt in Old Testament studies. Scholars who are skeptical about the results of historical criticism find the move to "the text itself" and a close reading of it to be a constructive one—thus the emphasis on rhetoric or poetic style.

This approach also reads the Bible as literature. Much of the history of interpretation would suggest that we read the Bible as "applied literature," literature for the purpose of communicating a theological message, rather than as "pure literature" read for pleasure.[6] The Bible certainly

---

[2]See Martin Kessler, "A Methodological Setting for Rhetorical Criticism," *Semitics* 4 (1974): 22-36; Clines, *I, He, We, & They*, 37; Isaac M. Kikawada, "Some Proposals for the Definition of Rhetorical Criticism," *Semitics* 5 (1977): 67-91; Weiss, "Total-Interpretation," 88-112, and "Neuen Dichtungswissenschaft," 255-302; David J. A. Clines, David M. Gunn, and Alan J. Hauser, eds., *Art and Meaning: Rhetoric in Biblical Literature*, JSOTSup 19 (Sheffield: JSOT Press, 1982).

[3]A number of the studies in the volume *Art and Meaning* were initially presented in the Rhetorical Criticism Section of recent Society of Biblical Literature meetings.

[4]See nn. 37-40 in chap. 1 and Cleanth Brooks, "The Formalist Critics," *Kenyon Review* 13 (1951): 72-81.

[5]See Lentricchia, *After the New Criticism;* Barton, *Reading the Old Testament*, 140-79. Barton has clearly chronicled the difficulties with the New Criticism. Nonetheless, we have already seen the convincing impact of the "intentional fallacy"; the interpreter has much to gain from a close reading of the text and its poetic style.

[6]See David Robertson, *The Old Testament and the Literary Critic*, GBS

contains literature of different sorts and purposes, but a dichotomy between a theological and a literary reading of the Bible is probably a false
one. The Old Testament certainly seeks to attract and persuade its readers
and thus confront them with the theological dimension. And Meir Sternberg has convincingly argued that a literary approach is consonant with
the types and purposes of Old Testament literature.[7] We will return to
this issue later.

From such a background, this chapter will look at the rhetoric of
Psalm 61. A definition of "rhetoric" can begin with Muilenburg's description of the task of rhetorical criticism as a study in literary composition, of the structural patterns and devices used to make up a whole literary unit,[8] in this case Psalm 61. However, such a study must be put in
the context of the "argument" of the whole text. Aristotle's classical definition of rhetoric is helpful in this context: "the art of discovering the
best possible means of persuasion in regard to any subject whatever."[9]
Our study will focus on the text's persuasive use of language and in that
context also move beyond structure to a more formal analysis of poetic
style and the psalm's literary devices. Characterization and plot are also
part of the psalm's persuasive use of language.

(Philadelphia: Fortress Press, 1977) 1-15; James Barr, "Reading the Bible as
Literature," *BJRL* 56 (1973): 10-33; and idem, *The Bible in the Modern World*,
53-74.

[7]Sternberg, *Poetics*, 1-57; see also McKnight, *The Bible and the Reader*.
Both Sternberg and McKnight, however, move further in the direction of the
reader. Robert Alter, "A Literary Approach to the Bible," *Commentary* 60
(1975): 70-77, argues for a literary approach more in line with this chapter.

[8]Muilenburg, "Form Criticism and Beyond," 8. For comment, see Dale
Patrick and Allen Scult, *Rhetoric and Biblical Interpretation*, JSOTSup 82 /
Bible and Literature Series 26 (Sheffield: Almond Press, 1990) 11-27.

[9]Aristotle, *Rhetoric* 1.1, quoted in Kessler, *Semitics* (1974): 22. Broyles, *Conflict of Faith and Experience*, 28-34, provides constructive comments on the analysis of rhetoric in this sense, in a form-critical context. Also helpful is the description of rhetorical criticism in George A. Kennedy, *New Testament
Interpretation Through Rhetorical Criticism*, Studies in Religion (Chapel
Hill/London: University of North Carolina Press, 1984) 3-38; also cf. Wellek and
Warren, *Theory of Literature*, 129-45.

Some may wonder about applying an Aristotelian notion of rhetoric, so often applied to narratives with a thread of continuity, to a psalm. Craig Broyles has suggested three categories of listeners/readers of the Psalms: God, the audience in the original setting, and those who have at hand only the text of the psalm.[10] The third category operates in continuity with the second and consists of generations of communities which have heard/read Psalm 61 and acknowledged its import. In that sense they have found the psalm persuasive. In its most basic form, the psalm seeks to persuade God. If rhetoric has to do with the use of language to achieve certain effects,[11] a rhetorical analysis is entirely appropriate for Psalm 61.

Structure

Our description of the structure of Psalm 61 considered matters of rhetoric;[12] another look at the main points of the structure is also integral to this chapter. The first verse is the superscription to the psalm and so outside the structure proper. Structural markers indicate the psalm's basic sections. A major break comes after v. 6. The prayer begins with שִׁמְעָה אֱלֹהִים, "Hear, O God"; the response comes in v. 6, כִּי־אַתָּה אֱלֹהִים שָׁמַעְתָּ, "Indeed, you, O God, have heard." A further division in vv. 2-6 is marked with כִּי (v. 4), indicating the motivation for the preceding prayer. So vv. 2-4 and vv. 5-6 comprise the first two sections of the psalm. The last verse paragraph, vv. 7-9, is marked off with the repetition יָמִים עַל־יְמֵי, "Days upon days" (v. 7), and יוֹם יוֹם, "day by day" (v. 9). A reminder of the style of each section might be helpful.

Verses 2-4 progress from the opening prayer for hearing, to the condition of trouble, through the plea for safety, to the affirmation that God has served as a refuge. The plea for hearing (v. 2) gains greater focus in the petition in v. 3, and v. 4 provides motivation for the prayer. The first common singular dominates, balanced with the second masculine singular. In this first verse paragraph, the speaker pleads for hearing and pro-

---

[10]Broyles, *Conflict of Faith and Experience*, 24-25.

[11]See Robert Con Davis and Ronald Schleifer, eds., *Contemporary Literary Criticism: Literary and Cultural Studies*, 2nd ed., Longman English and Humanities Series (New York: Longman, 1989) 67-73.

[12]See chap. 2.

tection in the face of the enemy, a plea based on past experience of God as strong fortress and refuge.

The second masculine singular dominates in vv. 5-6, and the focus shifts to the temple. The movement is from first common singular petition to second masculine singular response; v. 5 pleads for protection, and v. 6 speaks of response. The emphasis in v. 6 is on the fact that God has heard: כִּי־אַתָּה אֱלֹהִים שָׁמַעְתָּ, "Indeed, you, O God, have heard," a sign that the speaker is included in the community of faith—in contrast to the enemies mentioned at the end of v. 4. Verses 5-6 contrast the speaker with the enemies and thus bolster the argument that the petitioner should be among those receiving God's hearing, protection, and blessing. We have already noted the difficulties in interpreting v. 6.[13] This reading of the psalm's structure understands the verse as an expression of certainty that God hears the prayer. Verses 5-6, then, are made up of petition followed by hearing. Verse 6 makes the transition to the third verse paragraph of the psalm; the heritage given at the end of v. 6 leads to petition for the guarantor of that heritage, the king (vv. 7-8).[14]

The final section is set off with a clear marker, the use of "days upon days" beginning v. 7 and "day by day" concluding v. 9. Each verse seems to have a progression: from day to years to generations in v. 7; from enthronement to protection by God's חֶסֶד וֶאֱמֶת in v. 8; from praise forever to fulfilling vows daily in v. 9. The overall movement is from petition to vow of praise. The conclusion of the psalm is emphatic, beginning with כִּי and giving focus to praise and fulfilling vows on a daily basis. The conclusion is also a hopeful one, a hopeful one for the faithful worshiper, whose praise of God and fulfilment of vows goes on through life. The psalm pictures its protagonist as a petitioner who prays for the king and vows continued praise. So this last section is petition followed by vow.

We have already noted other possible descriptions of the psalm's structure. We have seen that one could interpret v. 6 not as an expression

---

[13]See chap. 2.

[14]Note the connections between v. 6 and v. 9, שְׁמֶךָ and נְדָרַי in v. 6 and שִׁמְךָ and נְדָרַי in v. 9, and the connections between v. 5 and v. 8: v. 5 speaks of protection for the speaker, and v. 8 of protection for the king; v. 5 uses עוֹלָמִים and v. 8 uses עוֹלָם.

of certainty but as a motivation for the prayer in v. 5. Vows could provide a motivation for answering petition, and the granting of "heritage"
could refer to God's past action. Verses 2-6 would then comprise a
double petition, each followed by motivation. Some interpreters describe
the psalm's structure as consisting of two parts: prayer (vv. 2-5) and expression of confidence (vv. 6-9).[15] We have already noted the connections
between v. 6 and what follows. The root חָסָה occurs in v. 4 and v. 5,
providing a connection between vv. 2-4 and v. 5. A final alternative
would consider vv. 2-3 as petition, vv. 4-5 as expression of trust followed
by a wish, v. 6 as expression of the certainty of a hearing, vv. 7-8 as
petition for the king, and v. 9 as vow.[16] Verse 4, beginning with כִּי,
would then introduce a request.

Each of these proposals emphasizes a particular aspect of the text and
warrants consideration. However, the first proposal of structure we have
considered in this chapter seems to take the fullest account of the psalm's
stylistic devices. It suggests that the psalm contains three sections (vv. 2-
4, 5-6, 7-9). The first is petition followed by motivation; the second is
petition followed by positive response. The final verse paragraph is petition for the king followed by vow. We will return to the implications of
this structure.

Poetic Form

Another crucial aspect of the psalm's rhetorical composition is the
poetic form embedded in its structure. Much work has appeared on
Hebrew poetry lately.[17] As we saw in the introductory chapter, scholars
have traditionally tied Hebrew poetry to some system of meter (perhaps
syllable count or the number of beats or accented units per line or the
length of a line) and parallelism. There does seem to be a limit to the
length of a line of Hebrew poetry and so probably something akin to
meter, but no one has satisfactorily described it.

---

[15]Delitzsch, *Biblical Commentary*, 229-30; Kirkpatrick, *Palms*, 344.

[16]See Gunkel, *Die Psalmen*, 260-61; Kraus, *Psalms 60-150*, 8; Anderson,
Psalms, 1:446-47.

[17]For a convenient summary, see Miller, *Interpreting the Psalms*, 16-17, 29-
47.

The current debate has centered on parallelism. Most traditional hand-books on Hebrew poetry would describe—in the tradition of Lowth—parallelism as each line in a verse presenting parallel thoughts, synonymous, antithetic, or synthetic. Most contemporary interpreters have moved in different directions.[18] How can we describe parallelism? In an influential study, James Kugel has described parallelism as a kind of echo effect, in which line A makes a statement and line B says, "Yes, and even more so this."[19] His work has made a real contribution to the study of Hebrew poetry. However, others would say parallelism defies such a simple description.[20] Kugel has even raised the question of whether we ought to make such a distinction between Hebrew prose and poetry. Most would still suggest that we should, and perhaps the foremost among such contemporary interpreters is Robert Alter. He notes that poetry is a succinct, highly structured means of expression and that it makes use of a variety of literary devices to engage the reader.[21] Alter expresses appreciation for Kugel's description of parallelism in terms of "seconding," but he suggests that the parallelism of Hebrew poetry is more dynamic in nature. He argues that the poems grow in specificity and intensity.

The Psalms certainly make use of conventional language, indeed are powerfully influenced by literary convention. There is much in common. At the same time, there is much variety. The psalmists exploit convention and exhibit a great variety of skill. Alter's perspective provides some constructive avenues for exploring this poetry of the Psalms. The poems use parallel structures on a variety of levels—matching words, phrases, lines, thought sequences—and a variety of other devices to involve the

---

[18]For the history of the issue, see Kugel, *Biblical Poetry*.

[19]Kugel, *Biblical Poetry*.

[20]See, e.g., Adele Berlin, *The Dynamics of Biblical Parallelism* (Bloomington: Indiana University Press, 1985); Stephen A. Geller, *Parallelism in Early Biblical Poetry*, HSM 20 (Missoula MT: Scholars Press, 1979); Alter, *Art of Biblical Poetry*.

[21]Alter, *Art of Biblical Poetry*. See also idem, "Psalms," 244-62; Wilfred G. E. Watson, *Classical Hebrew Poetry: A Guide to its Techniques*, JSOTSup 26 (Sheffield: JSOT, 1984); David Noel Freedman, "Another Look at Biblical Hebrew Poetry," in *Directions in Biblical Hebrew Poetry*, ed. Elaine R. Follis, JSOTSup 40 (Sheffield: JSOT, 1987) 11-28.

reader in the psalm's drama.[22] What can we say, from this perspective, about the poetry of Psalm 61?

The psalm begins with a kind of echo effect; line B seconds line A:

[2]Hear, O God, my cry;
    attend to my prayer.

From this introductory plea for hearing, the prayer becomes more specific. Verses 3-4 lead us through trouble to the plea for protection to the affirmation that God has protected in the past:

[3]From the end of the earth I call unto you
    when my heart is faint;
        lead me to a rock high beyond me,
[4]for you have been a refuge for me,
    a strong tower in the face of the enemy.

Verse 4 shows the dynamic of parallel lines. In the second line, "refuge" becomes the more powerful "strong tower," and the enemy is mentioned, the psalm's only mention of the enemy. Verse 5 seeks to bring the past experience of protection into the present for the petitioner. The lines are again parallel with the second enriching the plea with the image of refuge in the shelter of the wings:

[5]Let me sojourn in your tent always;
    let me take refuge in the shelter of your wings.

The psalm then makes a decisive turn at v. 6 with God's response. In the first line God hears, and in the second God gives. There is a relationship between the lines, but its nature is not easy to define.

[6]Indeed, you, O God, have heard my vows;
    you have given the heritage of those who fear your name.

Perhaps the giving of the "heritage of those who fear your name" is based upon the hearing. This appearance of the community of faith and

---

[22]See Berlin, *Dynamics of Biblical Parallelism*; Bellinger, *Psalms*, 12-14, 33-43. Note the comment of David J. A. Clines, "The Parallelism of Greater Precision," in *Directions in Biblical Hebrew Poetry*, 94, that the relation of poetic lines is unpredictable.

its inheritance leads to a broadening of the prayer to the community's leader, the king:

> [7]Add days upon days for the king,
>   his years as generation after generation.
> [8]May he be enthroned forever before God.
>   Appoint loyalty and trustworthiness that they may preserve him.

The second line of v. 7 continues from the first, intensifying the prayer. The same is true in v. 8; the second line is more specific about divine protection for the king. Verse 9 exhibits a similar kind of parallelism. The first line speaks of praise and the second specifies the setting of that praise:

> [9]Thus I will praise your name forever
>   as I fulfil my vows day by day.

The psalm concludes on a confident note. It looks to the future in terms of continuing praise of the God who hears and gives. The conclusion is an emphatic one, resolving the need at hand and looking to a hopeful future. Thus the poetry has artfully traversed the path from crisis to petition to hope in the context of the worshiping community. It has succinctly and dramatically brought its readers through trouble to safety.

The poetic form of Psalm 61 makes possible a dynamic unfolding of a pilgrimage from crisis to hope, and it does so with only sixteen lines of poetry. Such a powerful mode of communication offered much to ancient Israel's theologians.[23]

Additional Literary Features

The psalm also makes use of additional literary features.[24] Consider the following.

1. *Divine Names.* Psalm 61 uses a divine name three times. On each occasion it is אֱלֹהִים, "God," as one would expect in the Elohistic Psalter. One occurrence is in each verse paragraph of the text, support for our description of the psalm's structure. The first occurrence addresses God

---

[23]This poetic analysis is much in line with Alter's work in *Art of Biblical Poetry.*

[24]See Bellinger, *Psalms,* 33-43.

with the prayer for hearing, and the second occurrence speaks of God's response. The prayer partakes of the lament/response pattern. The third use of אֱלֹהִים is in v. 8, the prayer that the king continue to rule in the aura of God's presence. The king had a special relationship with God and provided a means for the community to fully experience God's blessing.

2. *Loaded Terms*. By "loaded terms" I mean those which carry special significance for the tradition of ancient Israel's faith, terms such as מִשְׁפָּט, צֶדֶק, and חֶסֶד. The first set of such terms comes in vv. 3-5. The petitioner asks God, "lead me to a rock" (v. 3). The rock is a place high away from danger, a safe place, as in Ps. 27:5. In v. 5 of Psalm 61, the tent and shelter come into view, clearly a reference to the sanctuary. The Old Testament also describes God as rock, and v. 4 speaks of God as refuge and strong tower (see Pss. 19:15; 28:1; 31:4; 62:3, 7-9; 71:3; 78:35; 89:27; 91:2, 9; 95:1; 144:1). Ps. 94:22 speaks of God as "the rock of my refuge" (לְצוּר מַחְסִי). So the faith tradition of ancient Israel knew well the description of God as rock and as the one who places the needy upon a rock of safety. The community's history bears witness to God as the one who leads to safety and as the rock of salvation.

The offering of prayers and vows (vv. 2, 6, 9) was also of special importance to the faith community and those terms are common in the Psalms. We have already seen that vows were a part of the lament tradition. The prayer comes "when my heart is faint" (v. 3). The heart represents the person and particularly the person's courage and will. In such a situation, one cries to God (Ps. 102:1).

Also worthy of note is the use in v. 8 of חֶסֶד וֶאֱמֶת. The prayer is that these two will watch over the king. חֶסֶד is God's constant loyalty, no matter what the circumstances are. אֱמֶת reflects the tradition that God has demonstrated trustworthiness; one can safely entrust life to God. The prayer is that such constant divine protection be with the king, an agent of blessing for the community.

All of these loaded terms add to the persuasiveness of the language of Psalm 61. The poem makes constructive use of ancient Israel's faith tradition, in a persuasive prayer addressed to God and heard/read by the worshiping community.

3. *Repetition*. Repetition of words or synonyms is significant in Hebrew poetry and often indicates emphasis. We have noted repetition

which marks the psalm's structure.[25] Of particular note is the use of כִּי in vv. 4, 6 and of יוֹם in vv. 7, 9 (to mark the last section). The analysis of structure in chapter two and in the first part of this chapter has noted additional repetition.

Especially significant is the call for God to hear (שִׁמְעָה אֱלֹהִים, v. 2), and God hears (אֱלֹהִים שָׁמַעְתָּ, v. 6). That repetition is central to the significance of the prayer. Related is the frequent use of the first common singular (twelve times) and the second masculine singular with reference to God (ten times). The "I" prays fervently to the "Thou." The prayer is for protection; note the two uses of the root חָסָה (vv. 4, 5). The protection is associated with the temple with the two references in v. 5, בְּאָהָלְךָ and בְּסֵתֶר כְּנָפֶיךָ. The use of נֶדֶר and שֵׁם in vv. 6, 9 may also be relevant to the association. The uses of עוֹלָם in vv. 5, 8 and לָעַד in v. 9 give further emphasis to the prayer. The prayer is an intense one. Its use of language, including repetition, exploits the conventions of persuasion.

4. *Imagery.* Poetry makes great use of images, and the Psalms are no exception. The imagery of the Psalter has often gripped the imagination.

Psalm 61 begins with the image of fainting. The lamenters in the Psalms were gripped by the power of death. Courage melts in the face of enemies and oppression; the trouble issues in the cry to God, an act characteristic of ancient Israel. "From the end of the earth I call to you when my heart is faint" (v. 3). The image speaks of wax melting, of isolation and doubt. The image of fainting is the base from which the prayer springs.

The imagery of the psalm quickly moves to the contrasting pole in the second line of v. 3, to the rock. We have already noted the use of this image elsewhere in the Psalter. The rock images strength which provides safety in the face of difficulty. The next verse pushes the image to God as refuge and strong tower. The tower is a bulwark, a strong shield against the enemy and against all the elements of chaos assailing the speaker. Judges 9:51 provides a narrative context for such a tower, and

---

[25]See also Sternberg's helpful treatment of repetition, *Poetics of Biblical Narrative*, 365-440. Robert C. Tannehill, "The Composition of Acts 3-5: Narrative Development and the Echo Effect," SBLSP 23 (1984): 238-40, describes various functions of repetition.

Prov. 18:10 supplies a vivid picture of the function of the tower. As strong tower, God provides protection, refuge, against the storms of life. A martial context may lie behind the image; the opposing army cannot conquer the tower. The king (vv. 7-8) may also be a symbol of such strength. Verse 5 pushes the image of the divine further toward the notion of protection with the tent and shelter of the wings. We have already noted the interpretation of this image in terms of the cherubim or the temple or the protecting wing of the bird.[26] No doubt the phrase could conjure up associations with all three, but the protection of the mother bird is perhaps the most telling. Divine protection brings nurture and protection in the face of trouble.

Verse 5 certainly associates this strength and protection with the sanctuary. It becomes, as well as the place of worship in Jerusalem, an image of protection, of "home," because of the powerful protecting presence of God there.[27] So the imagery of the psalm presents a close connection between God and temple in terms of strong protection. This imagery is central to the text.

Our look at the psalm's imagery has suggested that the psalm moves from the picture of fainting on the edge of chaos to the strong protection of God's wings. Walter Brueggemann has chronicled this movement, though he describes it as the movement from the Pit (Sheol) to the shelter of the wings.[28] The movement is the same in Psalm 61, and the text ends in confident protection. This brief look at some of the additional literary features in Psalm 61 shows that the text exploits ancient Israel's faith tradition, especially in terms of lament and response, to communicate this gripping move from crisis to hope.

Characterization

Characterization is more often associated with narrative than with poetry.[29] Nonetheless, the lament psalms have been considered in terms of

---

[26]See chap. 3.

[27]See Clements, *God and Temple*, on the history of the divine presence in ancient Israel.

[28]Walter Brueggemann, *Praying the Psalms* (Winona MN: Saint Mary's Press/Christian Brothers Publications, 1982) 39-49.

[29]Shlomith Rimmon-Kenan, *Narrative Fiction: Contemporary Poetics*, New

the three primary "characters" involved the texts: the speaker, the enemies, and God.[30] How does Psalm 61 describe each character? How do the descriptions contribute to the psalm's rhetoric?

1. *The speaker.* The "I" of the psalm begins in a situation of dire distress, of "fainting" on the edge of Sheol. The person then calls out to God and argues a case before the one who can grant genuine protection from the enemy and any other trouble at hand. The speaker knows that God is one who hears and so speaks of the current situation in the context of relation with God. The speaker's self-characterization is as one who calls upon God, as of one of the faithful—in contrast to the enemy. In the latter part of the psalm, the petitioner is also faithful, fulfilling vows and praying for God's chosen king. Verse 6 announces that God has heard the speaker's prayer and counted this one among "those who fear your name," the community of the faithful. The psalm characterizes the speaker, in contrast to the enemy, as within God's care and protection. Such characterization encourages faith in hearers/readers and adds to the argument that God respond to the prayer.

2. *The enemy.* Psalm 61 makes only one mention of the enemy (אוֹיֵב, v. 4). The verse describes God as "a strong tower in the face of the enemy." Thus the enemy is in opposition to the speaker; the picture is of attacking. Beyond that, we know nothing of the character of the enemy. The enemy simply constitutes a troubling presence.

3. *God.* The psalm's characterization of God is as one who can be addressed from a setting of crisis. The community's history has demonstrated God's loyalty (v. 4). The current crisis challenges that assertion, and the speaker addresses God in the hope of response. The latter part of the psalm implies that God does respond and protect. The characterization is thus hopeful, confident in God's strong protection. This picture of God also encourages divine response and a response of faith from the worshiping community.

Accents (London/New York: Methuen & Co., 1983) provides helpful insights on characterization as a network of traits communicated by speech, description, action and narration. See also Clines, *I, He, We, & They*, 37-49.

[30]See Claus Westermann, "Struktur und Geschichte der Klage im Alten Testament," *ZAW* 66 (1954): 44-80.

Other characters are also present. *The king* comes to the fore in vv. 7-8; the representation is of an ideal king. The rhetor hopes for a faithful and thus blessed king; such a king could be a means of blessing. In addition, *the community* is called "those who fear your name" in v. 6, and the speaker desires to be a part of that group.[31]

Plot

Our study of various aspects of the rhetoric of Psalm 61 has looked at the poem's stylistic devices as a means of bolstering the prayer's argument. What are our conclusions? We will consider them under the rubric of plot. Plot is also usually described, quite appropriately, in terms of narrative. Psalm 61 is, of course, a poetic prayer, but it has a plot in the sense that it begins with a conflict which is resolved.[32] It brings to expression crisis and response. This approach fits the lament psalms generally. They, along with the thanksgiving psalms, have a "narrative" quality about them.[33]

When I combine observations on structure, poetic form, and additional literary devices, I get a full picture of Psalm 61 as an artful piece of rhetoric. Consider its plot. The first section (vv. 2-4) presents a prayer for hearing and protection. Section two (vv. 5-6) continues that prayer and concludes with response. Section three (vv. 7-9) also gives expression to petition but widens the prayer to the king, leader of the community, and projects the psalm into the future praise of God.[34] Each section begins with petition and ends with hopeful affirmation. These affirmations increase in intensity. The first (v. 4) is motivation for God to answer, an

---

[31]The psalm's superscription also mentions David and the choirmaster. The psalm is from a Davidic collection and was used in a liturgical setting.

[32]See A. M. Vater, "Story Patterns for a *Sitz*: A Form- or Literary-Critical Concern?" *JSOT* 11 (1979): 48.

[33]Claus Westermann calls the thanksgiving psalms "narrative" or "declarative" psalms of praise (*Praise and Lament in the Psalms*, and *The Psalms: Structure, Content & Message*, trans. Ralph D. Gehrke [Minnneapolis: Augsburg, 1980]). See also Terence Collins, "Decoding the Psalms: A Structural Approach to the Psalter," *JSOT* 37 (1987): 53.

[34]If one favors an alternative description of the psalm's structure (see chap. 2, above) this summary of plot would shift somewhat, but the approach would not change.

affirmation of God's past protection. The second (v. 6) speaks of God's positive response to the prayer, and the third (v. 9) envisions future praise of God and fulfilling of vows. Each section builds on the preceding one and is somewhat distinct; the psalm moves through a clear sequence. Each petition moves forward to hopeful affirmation. The psalm begins with an emphasis on "I," moves to "you," God, and then expands to the whole community and the future. The psalm concludes with the speaker firmly within the safety of the faith community. The "you," God, relates to the "I" so that the worshiper, in contrast to the enemy, is included among the faithful.

The pivotal move is in section two (vv. 5-6), the move to divine response. This section centers on the refuge associated with the sanctuary, central to the resolution of the speaker's crisis and the granting of the "heritage." The specificity and intensity of the poem grow throughout vv. 2-6; after v. 6, the prayer broadens beyond the speaker's current circumstance. The text moves from fainting to sheltering protection to praise in the context of community, from Sheol to sanctuary to thanksgiving, from lament to divine response to human response. The characterizations of the speaker as faithful and of God as the one who hears add further emphasis to the prayer.

Psalm 61 uses all this rhetoric in the context of conflict with God. The immediate purpose of the prayer is to persuade God to protect the worshiper "in the face of the enemy" (v. 4). Verses 6, 9 bear witness to the resolution of the conflict. But the rhetoric also flows in another direction. It serves to persuade the hearing/reading community, both ancient and modern, to join with the speaker in addressing God in times of trouble and in claiming the declaration that God hears and responds to such prayers. The psalm thus nurtures faith. The rhetoric is bidirectional. God's response is affirmed; the community's awaited.

Another way to consider plot would be to construct the symbolic world or story behind the psalm. A starting point would be the psalm's characters and their relationships.

```
                        Speaker
                          ‖
      King————————————God————————————Enemy
                          │
                      Community
```

Each of the other characters has a direct relationship with God. God provides protection, refuge, and shelter for the speaker; and the speaker offers praise and fulfills vows to God. The community is characterized as those who fear God's name. The king is enthroned before God, and the prayer asks that God's loyalty and trustworthiness preserve the monarch. These protectors, almost personifications, come from God. And finally, God is "a strong tower in the face of the enemy." On this account, God is the central character in Psalm 61, and the relationship between God and the speaker is of particular note.

What are the relationships between the other characters? At this point, we encounter notable gaps in the text.[35] The enemy only appears once in the psalm and then with no pronominal suffix to indicate relationship to the speaker. God is a strong tower in the face of the enemy. From the context of the preceding line—God as a refuge for the speaker—I have inferred a contrast between speaker and enemy. Other psalms also provide support for filling the gap in that way. Similarly, I would infer a contrast between enemy and community along with king.

The speaker appears to be part of the community:

> Indeed, you, O God have heard my vows;
>> you have given the heritage of those who fear your name. (v. 6)

But notice that there is, in fact, no reference to the speaker in the second line of the verse. This gap has often puzzled commentators, but reading the text forces one to fill the gap. The king is leader of the community, but what is the relationship between the king and the speaker? This question has also exercised many interpreters. One possibility is that the king is the one who guarantees the speaker's place in the community. Such a view would account for the last line of v. 6 and the prayer for long life and protection for the monarch. Consider this charting of the web of relationships between the psalm's characters:

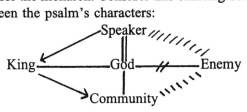

---

[35]See Sternberg, *Poetics of Biblical Narrative*, 186-229, 235-40.

In the psalm's symbolic world, God is the central actor, moving to protect king, community, and speaker against the enemy. The psalm pleads for such to happen. Constructing the psalm's symbolic world is reminiscent of the work of Paul Ricoeur who speaks of the world the text makes possible.[36] It is a metaphorical world, one created by the text, not a world of historical reference but of a new way of looking at things. Gaps call the reader to encounter that world; the reader will fill the gaps and thus conceive the world of the text. The symbolic world of Psalm 61 commends to the reader the God who protects and blesses. Thus the psalm nurtures faith.

I should make one final comment. I have not addressed the question of whether the rhetor and king are the same person. A shift takes place with the mention of the king in v. 7, and the psalm's rhetoric seems to leave the issue at that level. However, it is quite clear that this psalm would support Davidic ideology. The king is connected with the desired divine protection; and the use of such prayers, no doubt, engendered loyalty to the Davidic establishment in Jerusalem.[37]

Our analysis of rhetoric has used contemporary categories. George A. Kennedy has examined the categories of classical rhetoric.[38] A rhetorical analysis considers the rhetorical unit, rhetorical situation,[39] and rhetorical problem. Rhetoric appeals to an audience. Our psalm is likely epideictic and uses pathos with its audience as the persuasive mode. Kennedy also treats the arrangement and style of rhetorical texts. Our categories are different, but this chapter has considered each of the categories Kennedy discusses.

This look at the rhetoric of the psalm has provided essential information for the interpreter. The various aspects of the psalm's per-

---

[36]See n. 61 in the first chapter.

[37]See Wilhelm Wuellner, "Where Is Rhetorical Criticism Taking Us?" *CBQ* 49 (1987): 448-63.

[38]Kennedy, *New Testament Interpretation*, 3-38. See also E. A. Nida, J. P. Louw, A. H. Snyman, J. v. W. Cronje, *Style and Discourse: With Special Reference to the Text of the Greek New Testament* (Cape Town: Bible Society, 1983).

[39]This chapter on the psalm's rhetoric and chap. 3 on the psalm's setting relate to the rhetorical setting; see L. F. Bitzer, "The Rhetorical Situation," in *Rhetoric: A Tradition in Transition*, ed. W. R. Fisher (Ann Arbor: University of Michigan Press, 1974) 247-60.

suasive use of language come together in its purpose. Our examination of "the text itself" has been constructive. The chapter has methodically considered aspects of rhetoric, rather like the examination of a narrative, but the psalm is poetic. It is brief and has a kind of simultaneity to it. Readers can comprehend the impact of the rhetoric suddenly, but even such a response goes through a process.[40] The psalm's rhetorical effect is significant and affects the community in a variety of ways. We have examined those in the context of the psalm's persuasive purpose.[41]

Conclusion

This chapter has considered the rhetoric of Psalm 61.[42] The prayer is in three sections which move from petition to hope in a structure of intensification. The shift is from trouble to favorable divine response to praise of God. The conflict is resolved and faith nurtured. The psalm is quite persuasive indeed. This look at rhetoric provides a natural transition to the next stage in our journey with Psalm 61—a consideration of readers.

---

[40]On the importance of interpreting a poem "as a whole," see Broyles, *Conflict of Faith and Experience.*

[41]Patrick and Scult, *Rhetoric and Biblical Interpretation,* 11-44, and Edwin Black, *Rhetorical Criticism: A Study in Method* (Madison: University of Wisconsin Press, 1978) 10-17, note the significance of the notion of persuasion in rhetorical analyses. Remember the audiences: God, the original hearers, and later readers.

[42]"Rhetoric" often connotes a setting of public speaking. I have carried the term over to a written text; but in the ancient world, the text would have been read aloud and heard. The point is not that reading aloud is preferable but that oral performance probably creates an effect different from silent reading. See *Orality, Aurality and Biblical Narrative,* ed. Lou H. Silberman, *Semeia* 39 (Atlanta: Scholars Press, 1987).

Readers

Introduction

Our pilgrimage with Psalm 61 has taken us through two of the aspects of interpretation we discussed at the beginning of the project: origin and text. We now come to the third area of interpretation, the reader. Here the process of communication is completed. Biblical scholars have begun to give significant attention to the place of readers in the interpretive process. Much of the impetus for that move has come from developments in the broader field of literary criticism.

We have already had occasion to note, in chapters 1 and 4, the impact of the New Criticism on interpretation. It moved attention away from issues of origin and authorial intent to the text itself. The philosophical and literary movement structuralism has had a similar impact, primarily in European circles, in that it shifted attention away from concerns with origins. But structuralism has pushed the issue beyond the text to the reader; John Barton is correct in arguing that structuralism is at base a theory about reading texts.[1] We also saw in the introductory chapter, along with Jonathan Culler,[2] that structuralists have not given a lot of attention to poetry, perhaps because of the distinctive qualities of each work. We also noted there that the influence of structuralism has diminished in recent years. Nonetheless, the movement has left its mark on biblical studies. Its significance was explored, for example, in an issue

---

[1]Barton, *Reading the Old Testament*, 104-39.
[2]Culler, *Structuralist Poetics*, 161-88.

of the journal *Interpretation*,[3] and Barton has noted various works reflecting what he calls biblical structuralism.[4]

To come more directly to Psalm 61, Pierre Auffret has written two structuralist treatments of this text.[5] He notes various structures in the text—poetic and phonetic structures as well as the various connections between the parts of the text. He reads the text carefully and notices many possibilities for reading. His treatment of the psalm published in 1982 is quite complicated; the work of structuralists often seems obscure. While Auffret makes astute observations about the psalm, I wonder how many readers, other than Auffret—whether readers/hearers in ancient Israel or the contemporary world—would comprehend or come to such complicated readings. Auffret's 1984 article on the psalm presents a less complicated view.

More broadly, Terence Collins has articulated a structuralist approach to the Psalter.[6] He considers the various modes of discourse in the psalms and seeks to reduce a psalm to its various underlying statements or structures and group them according to patterns. The underlying narrative structure of the Psalter portrays God as helping the speaker in the face of opposition, as sending deliverance or blessing to the speaker. Various psalms partake of this basic structure. Collins's approach uses insights already a part of form-critical studies of psalms, but his work seems to homogenize psalms into a basic structure which fails to account for the rich diversity in this biblical book. Collins himself says that a structural analysis of the Psalter may seem a surprising thing to attempt.

My purpose here is not to present a full account of the influence of structuralist interpretation on Old Testament studies or to engage in a discussion of the merits of structuralism. Its influence seems to be waning, but it provides an important bridge to recent hermeneutical developments, especially reader-oriented criticism.

---

[3]*Interpretation* 28 (1974) included Robert C. Culley, "Structural Analysis: Is it Done with Mirrors?" 165-81; Richard Jacobson, "The Structuralists and the Bible," 146-64; and Robert A. Spivey, "Structuralism and Biblical Studies: The Uninvited Guest," 133-45.

[4]Barton, *Reading the Old Testament*, 121-39.

[5]Auffret, "Structure literaire de psaume 61," and "Étude structurelle du psaume 61."

[6]Collins, "Decoding the Psalms."

We have already noted the place given to the reader in contemporary literary-critical work. That is reflected in a variety of works.[7] Edgar McKnight has chronicled the rise of reader-response criticism in biblical studies and shows its relationship to structuralist theory.[8] Various biblical scholars have begun to consider the place of the reader in the interpretive process. One of the most significant works is that of Meir Sternberg.[9] His volume deals with narrative and does not treat all of the relevant issues, but it is still probably the most comprehensive treatment we have. His approach emphasizes the place of the reader as guided by the movement of the text. Devices such as point of view, perspective, repetition, and gaps guide the reader through narrative to an anticipated outcome. We shall return to Sternberg's approach.

Recent feminist and materialist readings of biblical texts are also part of the emergence of reader-response criticism. These works are different from Sternberg's more phenomenological approach. They derive more from the context of readers and questions they bring to the text. Such studies still show the significance of the reader in the contemporary hermeneutical debate.[10]

Central to that debate is the question of the locus of meaning. Traditional historical critics advocated original or authorial intent as the controlling locus of meaning. "Historical objectivity" provided the base for interpretion. However, the multiplicity of conclusions and the clear influence of regnant ideologies on interpretation have caused many to doubt that basic tenet. Scholars wonder how much we can recover of a text's origin and how helpful that reconstruction is for the hermeneutical task. Thus New Critics located meaning in the "text itself." Questions about the autonomy of the text from the reader and the multiplicity of interpretations pushed others to locate meaning in readers. "Readers make sense," says McKnight.[11] Stanley Fish argues that readers bring meaning to texts. "Interpretation is not the art of construing but the art of

---

[7]See the discussion of poststructuralism in chap. 1.

[8]McKnight, *The Bible and the Reader* and *Postmodern Use of the Bible.*

[9]Sternberg, *Poetics of Biblical Narrative.*

[10]See R. S. Sugirtharajah, ed., *Voices from the Margin: Interpreting the Bible in the Third World* (Maryknoll NY: Orbis Books, 1991).

[11]McKnight, *The Bible and the Reader*, 12, 133.

constructing. Interpreters do not decode poems; they make them."[12] I take the point that readers make sense out of texts, but it still seems to me that the locus of meaning is to be found somewhere in an interaction between text and reader. It is, after all, the text which one is reading and which leads one on in the interpretive task. Thus the text, coming from some original setting, provides the reader with help in making sense. Indeed, the text provides warrant for attention to readers. The persuasive devices used have the purpose of drawing readers into the text and taking them on pilgrimage. Biblical texts often address their readers and beckon to them to enter the story. Texts assume hearers or readers, and in reality people do read biblical texts. Thus, the text provides sufficient warrant for attention to the place of readers.

What do I mean by the "reader?" That issue is brought into better focus with the work of Seymour Chatman who speaks of real readers and of implied readers.[13] Those are readers we construct from the clues in the text, the text's characterization of the reader, "the audience presupposed by the narrative itself."[14] In some ways, we might more accurately use the term "inferred reader" because we construct a portrait of a reader from the text. When I speak of the reader, I am more interested in the related notion of informed readers, careful hearers/readers, of Psalm 61 in ancient Israel and through the generations. Much of what I say in this chapter is applicable to ancient readers, and much of my reading should be plausible for that setting. However, some of the issues I raise will come from the context of contemporary readers. Thus I work primarily with the notion of real readers, though I do infer things about the reader from the text. The reader in this chapter is thus the "informed reader," those competent to deal with the communication of the text.[15]

We will begin with the more phenomenological approach and explore the shape of reading Psalm 61. Then we will make the transition to a dis-

---

[12]Fish, *Is There a Text in This Class?* 327; see also Tzveton Todorov, "Reading as Construction," in *Reader in the Text*, 73.

[13]Seymour Chatman, *Story and Discourse: Narrative Structure in Fiction and Film* (Ithaca/London: Cornell University Press, 1978).

[14]Chatman, *Story and Discourse*, 150. Iser, *The Act of Reading*, 34, describes the implied reader as "a textual structure anticipating the presence of a recipient without necessarily defining him."

[15]See Fish, *Is There a Text in This Class?* 48-49.

cussion of matters related to the contemporary context of readers of the psalm.

The Reading Process

A number of centemporary literary critics speak of the process of reading. There are various constituents to the process; we will describe those and consider their relation to Psalm 61. This approach to reader response has a more phenomenological edge to it and has a significant background in critical theory. I have already mentioned the work of Seymour Chatman. He concentrates on how a narrative communicates its content or story. The "how" he labels "discourse," and he describes the various dimensions of that discourse. Note his diagram.[16]

Narrative Text

Implied →   Real →   (Narrator) →(Narratee) →Implied →   Real
Author   Author   Reader   Reader

A text might not include narrator or narratee; the implied author and reader are the picture the text portrays of author and reader. The text provides clues for the reader, guides for the reading process.

Wolfgang Iser is one of the significant theorists in this area. He describes reading in terms of the reader's transformation of signals sent by the text.[17] Various devices in the text influence the reader. The text offers schemas, but it is the convergence of text and reader which actualizes the literary work.[18] Shlomith Rimmon-Kenan has also contributed to our understanding of the reading process.[19] Reading is a dynamic process

---

[16]Chatman, *Story and Discourse*, 151. See also Wallace Martin, *Recent Theories of Narrative* (Ithaca NY/London: Cornell University Press, 1986) 154; and the works of Peter J. Rabinowitz: "Truth in Fiction: A Reexamination of Audiences," *Critical Inquiry* 4 (1977): 121-41; and idem, *Before Reading: Narrative Conventions and the Politics of Interpretation* (Ithaca/London: Cornell University Press, 1987).

[17]Iser, *Aspects of Narrative*, 3. See also Iser, *Act of Reading*, 107-34.

[18]Iser, *Implied Reader*, esp. 275.

[19]Rimmon-Kenan, *Narrative Fiction*.

in which the reader makes sense of the text. The various devices in the text invite the reader into that process.[20]

I have already noted Edgar McKnight's work.[21] He has traced the background of reader-oriented criticism through formalism and structuralism and the emphasis on the reader in Iser's work. He has concentrated on the relevance of this theory for biblical studies and has especially emphasized the role of the reader in contemporary biblical hermeneutics. He also speaks of readers actualizing the content of biblical texts through codes and structures. I have also already noted Meir Sternberg's work.[22]

Much of this work depends on an understanding of communication. An author produces a text to communicate with a reader. Thus reading completes the communication process; it is in the reception of the message that meaning is discovered. That is why we now have an emphasis on readers and readings of texts. The production of the text and its shape are certainly related to its meaning, but the reader actualizes it. That view is important for reading a psalm. What are the components of the reading process? I will describe some of them in relation to Psalm 61.

Beginnings. Iser speaks of a text prestructuring potential meaning; the reader actualizes such meaning. Thus a reader expects a text to move in certain directions. Sometimes those directions are unexpected, and the reader is also called upon to shift course.[23] The reader who comes to Psalm 61 already knows that a poetic text is at hand. That reality may shape expectations, even before reading begins. The informed reader of Psalm 61 may also come to the text knowing it is a lament and thus expect an honesty and boldness in addressing God. The beginning of the text may well confirm that view:

Hear, O God, my cry;
   attend to my prayer.
From the end of the earth I call unto you when my heart is faint.

---

[20]Rimmon-Kenan, *Narrative Fiction*, 118, describes the reader as "both an image of certain competence brought to the text and a structuring of such a competence within a text."

[21]McKnight, *The Bible and the Reader*. He treats Iser on 78-82, 122-24. See also McKnight, *Postmodern Use of the Bible*.

[22]Sternberg, *Poetics of Biblical Narrative*.

[23]Iser, *Implied Reader*, xii, 46.

No doubt, the variety of readings of the text relate to reader expectation. A view of the Psalms as pious, devotional language could color one's interpretation of Psalm 61, as could a view of the Psalms as brutally honest dialogue with God, a kind of calling God to task. Reader expectations are certainly part of the reading process.

Beginnings often determine expectations as the reader moves through the text. The opening of the text moves the reader from the real world into a perspective of the text.[24] The beginning of a text gives the reader a first impression. Edward Said describes the beginning as "the first step in the intentional production of meaning."[25] The beginning of Psalm 61 makes clear that the text will be a cry for help and the reader will expect a condition of crisis. The speaker, and thus the reader, clearly begin on the margin, on the edge of what counts as life.

The informed reader may well look forward (prospection) to an exposition of that condition and a move toward help. That expectation will take various turns in the text, but the beginning of the psalm certainly shapes the reading process.[26]

Sequence. Sequence has to do with the order in which the action moves in the text. Sequence seems a better word for poetry than does plot. If the speaker and reader begin on the margins of life, the move is through a plea "from the end of the earth" and a cry for refuge to a word of hope. The sequence then moves beyond the speaker to the king and thus calls the reader beyond the current circumstances of plea. Psalm 61 concludes with the vow of praise.

> Hear, O God, my cry;
>   attend to my prayer.
> From the end of the earth I call unto you when my heart is faint;

---

[24]See Boris Uspensky, *A Poetics of Composition: The Structure of the Artistic Text and Typology of a Compositional Form*, trans. Calentina Zavarin and Susan Wittig (Berkeley: University of California Press, 1973) 137; Mikeal C. Parsons, "Reading a Beginning/Beginning a Reading: Tracing Literary Theory on Narrative Openings," in *How Gospels Begin*, ed. Dennis E. Smith, *Semeia* 52 (Atlanta: Scholars Press, 1990) 11-31.

[25]Edward W. Said, *Beginnings: Intention and Method* (New York: Basic Books, 1975) 5.

[26]See Rimmon-Kenan, *Narrative Fiction*, 120.

lead me to a rock high beyond me,
for you have been a refuge for me,
a strong tower in the face of the enemy.
Let me sojourn in your tent always;
let me take refuge in the shelter of your wings.
Indeed, you, O God, have heard my vows;
you have given the heritage of those who fear your name.
Add days upon days for the king,
his years as generation after generation.
May he be enthroned forever before God;
appoint loyalty and trustworthiness that they may preserve him.
Thus I will praise your name forever
as I fulfil my vows day by day.

The "plot" is self-narrated, and thus the sequence operates from the point of view of the speaker and asks the reader to move with the speaker through the same sequence. It is more a sequence of spiritual pilgrimage rather than actions: the plea for refuge "from the end of the earth," the hope of divine response, and the prayer for the king and vow of praise.

Sequence is related to time. Time has to do with past, present, and future and the duration of time spent in each.[27] Time is interesting in the movement of Psalm 61. The psalm appears to begin in the present and stay there through v. 5. The crisis is at hand and issues in a plea for divine help. Verse 6 is the pivot of the psalm and implies divine aid as certain, as completed action. Verses 7-9 move to the future with the petition for the king and vow of praise. If v. 6 reflects a true expression of certainty, it also speaks of future time. The question of the relation of time in the text to time in the events reflected may also provide insight. The text stays in present and future. The events are only present. It does not appear that past events are narrated, except for the motivation for the prayer in v. 4. God's past protection is a basis for renewed protection in the crisis at hand.

Sequence is certainly important for the informed reader. The time relations in the process of reading the psalm provide additional insights for understanding.

---

[27]Ibid., 43-58. See also Chatman, *Story and Discourse*, 62-79; R. Alan Culpepper, *The Anatomy of the Fourth Gospel* (Philadelphia: Fortress Press, 1983) 50-75.

Focalization. The speaker of Psalm 61 maintains a certain perspective or point of view from which the sequence is narrated. Following Rimmon-Kenan, I prefer the term "focalization" as more inclusive.[28] Focalization indicates the focus from which one sees the action in a text. The text narrates a "plot" but it may do so from a variety of perspectives. Focalization may be inside the story or outside it.[29] If the narrator tells the story, the focalization is external to the story; the reader hears about the narrative. The focalization may, however, be from the perspective of one of the characters and thus internal to the described events.[30] The process of focalizing begins to draw the reader into the action of the events, and continues to take the reader through the narrative until the text's conclusion, at which point the reader leaves the narrative.[31]

The issue of focalization is interesting in Psalm 61 because of the self-narration involved. The speaker tells the story, a journey through spiritual dimensions of a crisis. Focalization, at least through v. 6, is internal to the action. The speaker calls the reader to pray alongside in the journey through trouble and to remember God's past help. The reader participates in the plea and the relief at the hope of response. Such is also true of the psalm's last verse. Verses 7-8 shift the focus somewhat to the king. On the whole, however, the focalization of the text calls the reader to join the speaker in the journey through pain to hope.

Characterization. We considered characterization in chapter 5 but it is also relevant to the reading process.[32] Characterization is often associated with narrative, but there is a sense in which the speakers, enemies, and God are characters in the Psalms. Rimmon-Kenan identifies characterization as a network of traits communicated by speech, description,

---

[28]Rimmon-Kenan, *Narrative Fiction*, 71. See also Chatman, *Story and Discourse*, 153; Uspensky, *Poetics of Composition*, esp. 6.

[29]See Rimmon-Kenan, *Narrative Fiction*, 72.

[30]See Mikeal C. Parsons, *The Departure of Jesus in Luke-Acts: The Ascension Narrative in Context*, JSNTSup 21 (Sheffield: JSOT Press, 1987) 101-102, 178-80; Gerald Prince, *Narratology: The Form and Functioning of Narratives* (New York: Mouton, 1982) 51-52.

[31]See Robert W. Funk, *The Poetics of Biblical Narrative* (Sonoma CA: Polebridge, 1989) 24.

[32]Chap. 5 looked at both characterization and plot from a "text-immanent" perspective. This chapter considers them from the perspective of the reader.

action, and narration.[33] The Psalms certainly portray speakers, enemies, and God through these media.

The speaker's self-characterization in Psalm 61 is as one who calls upon God, as one of the faithful fulfilling vows and praying for God's chosen king. Verse 6 characterizes the speaker as partaking of God's care and protection. In turn, the text characterizes God as one who can be addressed from crisis and one who has helped in the past (v. 4). The characterization is hopeful, even in the midst of crisis. Enemies, king, and community also come into view, but speaker and God are the major characters. They are portrayed briefly but vividly. Characterization is certainly one dimension of reading a psalm.

Gaps. A text does not provide everything for readers. Sternberg says a "literary work consists of bits and fragments to be linked and pieced together in the process of reading: it establishes a system of gaps that must be filled."[34] Shlomith Rimmon-Kenan suggests that the text draws the reader in with delays in the action and with gaps. Readers keep guessing. Gaps may thus be temporary, or they may be permanent. Rimmon-Kenan also says gaps may be prospective, that is, the reader is aware of the gap, or retrospective, that is, the reader is not aware of the gap until it is filled. Gaps enhance the interest and curiosity of readers.[35] That view also fits well with Iser's.[36] Indeed, Iser sees gaps as the central link in communication. Readers take language apart and put it back together. This "putting back together," the filling of gaps by the reader, is the beginning of communication. The reader provides a frame to link the parts of the text and begin interpretation.

> What is concealed spurs the reader into action, but this action is also controlled by what is revealed. . . . Whenever the reader bridges the

---

[33]Rimmon-Kenan, *Narrative Fiction*, 29-42. See also Chatman, *Story and Discourse*, 119; Martin, *Recent Theories of Narrative*, 116-22.

[34]Sternberg, *Poetics of Biblical Narrative*, 186.

[35]Rimmon-Kenan, *Narrative Fiction*, 125-29. See also Shlomith Rimmon, *The Concept of Ambiguity—The Example of James* (Chicago: University of Chicago Press, 1977) 47ff.

[36]Iser, *The Implied Reader*, 58, 280; *The Act of Reading*, 169-70, 202-203; and *Aspects of Narrative*, 1-45.

gaps, communication begins. The gaps function as a kind of pivot on which the whole text-reader relationship revolves.[37]

The filling of gaps grows as one moves through a text.[38] Readers fill gaps to seek coherence in the narrative, and the text gives clues to the appropriate filling of gaps.[39]

Psalm 61 tells readers of being gripped by the power of Sheol. There is never any specific definition of the crisis at hand. That permanent gap enables readers to enter the text with the narrator and appropriate the prayer for use in similar crises. Verse 3 pleads for help; the nature of that help is further defined in v. 5, protection related to the sanctuary. Gaps then play a major role in reading the rest of the psalm. The last line of v. 6 leaves readers to fill in gaps. What is the "heritage?" I have filled the gap in terms of membership among "those who fear thy name," the community of the faithful. We have already noted other interpretive possibilities. We have also noted that the whole of v. 6 is ambiguous. Is it, as I have suggested, an expression of certainty that God hears the prayer, or is it further motivation for the plea? I have filled the gap on the basis of the movement of the psalm and by comparison with other psalms of lament. Another significant gap comes between v. 6 and v. 7. How does the reader make the transition from the speaker in the first part of the psalm to the prayer for the king and back to the speaker in v. 9? I would suggest that the king as the leader of the community is the guarantor of the protection sought. Others would argue that the king is the speaker in the whole of the psalm.

The most significant point here is the awareness of gaps and that readers fill them. Readers are making sense of the text. That is a necessary part of the reading process. Awareness of gaps and of the basis on which readers fill in the blanks is valuable in the interpretive task.

Intertextuality. This dimension of the reading process has received much notice recently. The term derives from the work of Julia Kristeva who suggests that every text builds itself from other texts. I use the term to speak of the relation of a text with other texts in the hope that noting

---

[37]Iser, "Interaction Between Text and Reader," *The Reader in the Text*, 111.
[38]See McKnight, *The Bible and the Reader*, 79-80.
[39]Sternberg, *Poetics of Biblical Narrative*, 189.

such relationships will enhance our reading of the text at hand. An intertextual reading will consider Psalm 61 in light of other texts.[40]

For the informed reader of the Psalter, perhaps the most natural intertextual relationship for our psalm is other laments.[41] The text echoes other cries for help; the similarities in vocabulary with Psalms 62 and 63 are striking. The first half of the Psalter is dominated by cries for help with similar movement, vocabulary, and theology. But another intertextual relation is important within the Psalter also—that to the psalms of praise. I have already noted the relation to the thanksgiving psalms through the vow of praise. But what about the hymns of praise? There God is described as the one who delivers.

> Yet thou art holy,
>> enthroned on the praises of Israel.
> In thee our fathers trusted;
>> they trusted, and thou didst deliver them.
> To thee they cried, and were saved;
>> in thee they trusted, and were not disappointed. (Ps. 22:4-6)[42]

Ps. 46:6 says that God will help Zion early. Laments such as Psalm 61 are in a sense a challenge to that tradition of praise to God as the one

---

[40]See Jeanine Parisier Plottel, "Introduction," in *Intertextuality: New Perspectives in Criticism*, ed. Jeanine Parisier Plottel and Hanna Charney, New York Literary Forum 2 (New York: New York Literary Forum, 1978) xiv-xx; Fish, *Is There a Text in This Class?* 65. Michael Fishbane, *Biblical Interpretation in Ancient Israel* (Oxford: Clarendon Press, 1984); and J. Severino Croatto, *Biblical Hermeneutics: Toward a Theory of Reading as the Production of Meaning*, trans. Robert R. Barr (Maryknoll NY: Orbis, 1987) 43-46, 89, suggest an intratextual approach for the Bible. See also W. H. Bellinger, Jr., "The Psalms and Acts: Reading and Rereading," *With Steadfast Purpose: Essays on Acts in Honor of Henry Jackson Flanders, Jr.*, ed. Naymond H. Keathley (Waco TX: Baylor University, 1990) 127-43, for another application of intertextuality. Various literary critics have noted the value of intertextual perspectives: Harold Bloom, *A Map of Misreading* (New York: Oxford, 1975); Jonathan Culler, *The Pursuit of Signs* (Ithaca NY: Cornell University Press, 1981) 104.

[41]See Robert C. Culley, *Oral Formulaic Language in the Biblical Psalms*, Near and Middle East Series 4 (Toronto: University of Toronto Press, 1967).

[42]Psalm 22 is of course a lament, but the quote still reflects the hymnic traditions.

who delivers. They cry to the God who has not delivered. They seek to make sense out of a reality not in line with the traditions of praise. They seek the God who can come to deliver.

That intertextual insight leads to another. The speaker in Psalm 61 calls for God to "hear" (שמע). That word echoes another famous text from the Hebrew Bible, Deuteronomy 6, which calls ancient Israel to "hear" (שמע). Many biblical texts are concerned with the "hearing," the obedience and faithfulness, of the people. When informed readers remember such texts, they can see that in a sense a lament like Psalm 61 is concerned with God's faithfulness and "hearing" the cry. God is here called to fulfill the divine part of the agreed relationship. God is called to deliver as the tradition affirms that God will.

These brief comments show that attention to intertextuality can open new interpretive possibilities for readers.

Closure. We have already noted the significance of prospection for the reading process. Retrospection is also significant. When readers move through a text, they begin to put its parts together. As they move further, they will often modify their interpretation based on the new dimension of understanding that unfolds as the action moves forward. Rimmon-Kenan describes reading as a dynamic process in which readers come to a finalized hypothesis by way of retrospective patterning. Readers make sense of texts by forming, modifying and replacing hypotheses as they progress through the narrative. Readers construct, transform and dismantle interpretive frames.[43] Iser also notes the importance of retrospection.[44] Progress in the reading process enables the reader to look back and more fully interpret the text.

The reference to God's past protection in Ps. 61:4 provides a broader context for the opening plea. That is also true of the plea in v. 5. It gives a more specific context in relation to the sanctuary. Verse 6 puts the entire plea in the context of God's gracious hearing of the cry. The setting further shifts with the introduction of the king in vv. 7-8 and with the

---

[43]Rimmon-Kenan, *Narrative Fiction*, 117-19. Also see Sternberg, *Poetics of Biblical Narrative*, 225.

[44]Iser, *The Implied Reader*, 282, 290, and *The Act of Reading*, 111-12. See also Michael Riffaterre, *Semiotics of Poetry*, Advances in Semiotics (Bloomington/London: Indiana University Press, 1978) 4-6.

vow in the concluding verse. In retrospect, the reader sees the psalm as a vivid movement from the Pit, the edge of death (v. 3), to the shelter of the wings and the concomitant joy. Real pain is put in a broader context.

The end of a text provides some form of closure for the reading process and thus final retrospection. Barbara Herrnstein Smith claims,

> Closure occurs when the concluding portion of a poem creates in the reader a sense of appropriate cessation. It announces and justifies the absence of further development; it reinforces the feeling of finality, completion, and composure which we value in all works of art; and it gives ultimate unity and coherence to the reader's experience of the poem by providing a point from which all the preceding elements may be viewed comprehensively and their relations grasped as part of a significant design.[45]

Mikeal Parsons has provided an interesting survey of recent works on closure in fiction and points to the model of Marianna Torgovnick.[46] Torgovnick is concerned with a conclusion's relation to the rest of the work, to the reader, and to the author as well as the point of view and focalization at the end of the work. Some endings clearly recall the beginning of the work (circularity); others refer to various points in the text (parallelism). Other endings are more open, linking more to future works than to the text at hand (linkage) or omitting a crucial element (incompletion).[47]

In one sense, the ending of Psalm 61 does call to mind its beginning. The psalm opens with a cry for help and closes with another address to God in mind, but an address of future praise. The circularity is really thus a kind of anticircularity. The reference to vows in v. 9 parallels that in v. 6. God will continue to hear vows of praise and thanksgiving for deliverance. Thus, using Torgovnick's terms, Psalm 61 does close coherently. At the same time, there is an openness in the ending of the psalm. Read in the context of the Psalter, the prayer links closely with psalms of thanksgiving. The vow in v. 9 leads to the praise and thanksgiving

---

[45]Barbara Herrnstein Smith, *Poetic Closure*, 36. See also Rimmon-Kenan, *Narrative Fiction*, 18; Marianna Torgovnick, *Closure in the Novel* (Princeton: Princeton University Press, 1981) 6.

[46]Parsons, *The Departure of Jesus in Luke-Acts*, 66-71.

[47]Torgovnick, *Closure in the Novel*, 13-14. The category of "incompletion" seems less relevant for Psalm 61, though see above on "gaps."

offered in those texts. The closure is thus similar to that of many laments but is closely related to other psalms to come, thanksgiving psalms. In that sense, the closure in Psalm 61 is open or ambiguous. It might be said to be closure and anticlosure.[48] Hope and relief are certainly at hand as is future praise and thanksgiving. The end of the psalm implies an ongoing pilgrimage with pain and thanksgiving also in the future. Expectation and dialogue remain. In that sense, I suspect that the psalm's closure is convincing and satisfying for readers, though not without effort.

The ending of the psalm completes the construct of the frame for reading.[49] The reader moves gradually from the journey through pain to hope and back to life. The future and continuing fulfillment of vows of praise are in the forefront of consciousness.

This discussion of the entire process of reading, a kind of poetics of Psalm 61, should encourage greater intentionality in reading and interpreting a psalm. That gain is a significant one. Some may question, though, the relevance of poetics as an approach to biblical psalmody. This approach is most often tied to narrative. I have assumed that, as Alter says, there is a narrative impulse to biblical poetry.[50] I have also reflected the view, long held by form critics, that there is a significant typicality to the Psalms. Thus one can meaningfully speak of the poetics of biblical psalmody. I readily admit that what I have done is more easily tied to laments and thanksgiving psalms, psalms more expressly akin to narrative. But what I have described can also inform one's reading of other kinds of psalms.[51]

---

[48]See Fisch, *Poetry with a Purpose*, 134, 149; D. A. Miller, *Narrative and its Discontents: Problems of Closure in the Traditional Novel* (Princeton: Princeton University Press, 1981).

[49]See n. 24 above; Parsons, *The Departure of Jesus in Luke-Acts*, 96-101; and Funk, *Poetics of Biblical Narrative*, 60.

[50]Alter, *Art of Biblical Poetry*, esp. 28.

[51]A true poetics of Psalm 61 would attend to the cultural codes reflected in the text: the significance of "the end of the earth," the tent, the king, vows. Of particular importance would be an understanding of the psalm's Hebrew poetry and its performance. I attended to these issues in earlier chapters, esp. 2 and 4.

The Context of the Reader

Up to this point, I have concentrated on a more phenomenological reader-oriented approach to Psalm 61. Other reader-response critics would suggest that we begin from the context of real readers rather than construct a reading process from the text. Readers do respond to the text in terms of its ideology. We have already noted feminist and materialist readings of texts. Those readings begin from the context of real readers and tend to suggest that the locus of meaning is in the reading community rather than in the text itself or in the text's origin. Some such readings focus on ancient readers, but many are oriented to modern, contemporary readers. The perspectives of both ancient and modern readers are legitimate. I am not unaware of the matter of constructing the ideology of ancient readers. Chapters 2 and 4 noted its relevance for Psalm 61, and it relates to the following section. However, I will concentrate on contemporary readers. Consider two significant issues which could shape one's reading of Psalm 61. These two issues will illustrate readings with rootage in the context of the reader.

Gender. Feminist readings have become a major force in contemporary American biblical scholarship.[52] They appropriately raise questions about patriarchal ideology reflected in texts from the Hebrew Bible. Certainly one of the places that issue arises is ancient Israel's cult. It was likely available to males and operated by a male priesthood. In that sense it was exclusive and legitimated a society dominated by patriarchy. In turn, it might be suggested that the God of the Psalms is also imaged as male.

What of Psalm 61? The patriarchy of the cult is probably reflected in the superscription with the masculine participle (the choirmaster) and

---

[52]See, e.g., Letty M. Russell, ed., *Feminist Interpretation of the Bible* (Philadelphia: Fortress Press, 1985); Adela Yarbro Collins, ed., *Feminist Perspectives on Biblical Scholarship*, Biblical Scholarship in North America (Chico CA: Scholars Press, 1985); Elizabeth Schüssler Fiorenza, *In Memory of Her: A Feminist Theological Reconstruction of Christian Origins* (New York: Crossroad, 1983) and *Bread Not Stone: The Challenge of Feminist Biblical Interpretation* (Boston: Beacon Press, 1984); Phyllis Trible, *God and the Rhetoric of Sexuality*, OBT (Philadelphia: Fortress Press, 1978) and *Texts of Terror: Literary-Feminist Readings of Biblical Narratives*, OBT (Philadelphia: Fortress Press, 1984).

reference to the Davidic collection. The reference to the king is significant. We noted in the last chapter that the text's rhetoric would support
Davidic ideology, certainly a patriarchal move. The psalm could be used
for social control in that direction. But, interestingly, after the superscription, the only mention of male gender is the king in vv. 7-8. One of the
advantages to the self-narration is that the speaker uses first-common-
singular forms, thus leaving gender not defined. The cult was patriarchal,
but the truth is that we do not know the gender of the speaker. I would
also argue that God is not given a gender in the text. God is addressed,
and the second masculine singular is used in vv. 3-6, 9. Given the structure of the Hebrew language, that usage reflects the culture's patriarchy
more than it proclaims a view of the gender of God. Two images of God
are interesting. The image of the "strong tower" in v. 4 may reflect a
martial background; and so many, though not all, readers would associate
it with male ideology. Nevertheless, in the Song of Solomon, "tower"
imagery appears always with the woman rather than the man (4:4; 7:5;
8:10).[53] Furthermore, in v. 5, one way to read the second line of the verse
has to do with the image of the mother bird, a feminine image. Psalm 61
does not assign God a masculine gender (nor a feminine one either, for
that matter).

Indeed, one could read the psalm quite positively on the contemporary issue of gender. Nothing should keep contemporary readers from
making the hermeneutical shift to view cult in a more inclusive way. In
fact, a more materialist reading of the text would see it as a plea for
inclusion. The speaker is excluded from the cult and from the "heritage"
(land?) of the community (v. 6) and implores the inclusive God to help
and embrace this one who has been marginalized—perhaps by patriarchy—in terms of community and goods. The king should guarantee such
hope. While more extensive treatments to "rehabilitate" may be needed,
it is possible to read Psalm 61 positively from the perspective of gender.
The issue and the angle, however, derive from the context of the reader,
likely a modern reader. If that reader seeks a negative outcome, the text
will also oblige. My view is that the reception of the text through the
centuries has seen it in a more nurturing light.

---

[53]See Carol Meyers, "Gender Imagery in the Song of Songs," *HAR* 10
(1987): 209-23.

God Language. I have considered God language from the inclusive/exclusive perspective, but perhaps an even more fundamental issue is whether any theistic reference is a serious possibility. Again, the issue arises from the contemporary setting. Because of our cultural context and reading of history, some would say we cannot so easily address "God" or assume "God." Psalm 61 does assume God, as does the Hebrew Bible, and it addresses God in the midst of a crisis. The speaker seeks to make the crisis God's also. The psalm operates out of a faith in which one does not move beyond the possibility of addressing God; the psalm is an act of hope.[54] It asks God to act as "God" does—to deliver—and the text ends on a positive note. Harold Fisch suggests that the Psalms are dialogical.[55] In a sense, the text is an inner dialogue, but there are limits to that journey into subjectivity. The text also relates to the cultic community. The "I" of the psalm, as a part of the community, exists in relationship to God; and it is in the poem that an encounter with God is possible, an encounter which creates a change in life. In that sense, the prayer was creative for the speaker and has continued to be for many hearers/readers through the centuries.

A contemporary reader who is dismissive of God language could well argue that Psalm 61 is an irrelevant relic of an ancient past and is to be ignored. However, a contemporary reader aware of the difficulty of God language might also see the text as a search for "God," an honest search in the midst of trouble, a search inward and outward, a search for some sense and anchor in the midst of chaos. That search is part of a tradition, a tradition with limits, but one which has nurtured many. Any search needs a tradition, and contemporary readers can learn from the search narrated or created in Psalm 61.

Psalm 61

This chapter has explored various dimensions of reader-oriented interpretations of Psalm 61. It might be helpful to pull them together briefly.

An informed reader will be expecting some sort of plea for help at this point in the Psalter. That plea begins from the edge of the world. One hears echoes of other laments and their pain and looks forward. The

---

[54]See Brueggemann, *Praying the Psalms*, 39-49.
[55]Fisch, *Poetry with a Purpose*, 104-35.

text moves fairly quickly to Yahweh's past protection and calls for protection in Yahweh's house. The text calls the reader to stand alongside the speaker in the present trouble. The emphasis shifts to hope in v. 6 and the latter part of the text gives a hopeful context for the prayer. The text closes looking forward to the future fulfilling of vows to God. The speaker has called God to task for not delivering or freeing or "hearing" and the call is heard. This reading of the psalm has filled gaps as we have noted above. The God of the hymns of praise, the God who delivers and blesses, acts benevolently. The speaker has been included in the community of order, moved from the margin to the tent or shelter, the center of renewal. The search is fruitful. But will the "I" stay among the blessed? The future is always uncertain. Note the "thus" beginning v. 9. With divine protection and royal guarantee of justice, there is order; but the future is always in question and the journey never static.

Conclusion

This chapter has traced the movement of method through structuralism to reader-response approaches. Attention to readers is important, and we have considered various methodological avenues here. We considered a more phenomenological approach and looked at the various elements in the reading process. We also considered issues originating from the reader's context and related these issues to Psalm 61. I have simply illustrated reader-oriented approaches, not commented on all the possibilities. I am especially concerned about method, and attention to the perspective of readers certainly enriches our journey with Psalm 61.

I will conclude with reflections on method and hermeneutics, but first we shall consider theological dimensions in the psalm.

Theology

Introduction

Our final consideration of Psalm 61 from a particular point of view will be a theological one. By theology I simply mean a look at the faith the psalm commends, at God and God's relationship to human beings and what that relationship implies. Even a surface reading of the psalm beckons one to reflect on such issues. The text clearly speaks of God and of the worshiper's relationship with God. That is true of the Psalter as a whole and of the Old Testament which is finally a theological document. Psalm 61 speaks in theological language. It calls for inquiry into its proclamation.

Our approach will be in tandem with other work done on Old Testament theology.[1] In particular, Claus Westermann has called for theological reflection closely tied to the way the Old Testament speaks of God's involvement with the world.[2] Such an emphasis characterizes most of the works on Old Testament theology since the revival of interest in the subject during this century. The Old Testament does not systematize

---

[1]For the history of this "discipline," see Clements, *A Century of Old Testament Study*, 118-40; H. Reventlow, *Problems in Old Testament Theology in the Twentieth Century* (Philadelphia: Fortress Press, 1985); G. Hasel, *Old Testament Theology: Basic Issues in the Current Debate*, 3rd ed. (Grand Rapids: 1972); J. Hayes and F. Prussner, *Old Testament Theology: Its History and Development* (Atlanta: John Knox Press, 1985); W. Brueggemann, "A Convergence in Recent Old Testament Theologies," *JSOT* 18 (1980): 2-18.

[2]See esp. Claus Westermann, *What Does the Old Testament Say About God?* ed. F. W. Golka (Atlanta: John Knox Press, 1979); idem, *Elements of Old Testament Theology*, trans. Douglas W. Stott (Atlanta: John Knox Press, 1982).

or even organize its theology; nonetheless it is possible to investigate its main emphases. The same is true of the Psalter.[3]

Also of help is the work of Paul Ricoeur.[4] He seeks to call us beyond the "desert of criticism" to the world which the text makes possible.[5] It is a metaphorical world created by the text, not a world of historical reference but of a new way of looking at things.[6] The text mediates a world which intersects with the world of the reader in the hope that the reader's world will thereby be enlarged. Such a process of interpreting a text brings self-understanding and new modes of life.[7] The text makes possible a new theological world, one which gives life. How can we portray the world of Psalm 61? What are its primary themes or images?

Theological Themes

1. What is God doing in the text? Elizabeth Achtemeier says that if we do not speak to this question, we have nothing to say about the gospel.[8] We have already noted the prominence of God language in the text. Psalm 61 addresses God in the midst of trouble. Its affirmations (vv. 4, 6, 9) attest to God as strong tower and refuge, as the one who hears, as the one worthy of praise. Such statements push the description of God's activity toward that of providence. History has shown God to be worthy of trust (אֱמֶת).[9] God is the one who hears and responds. Consider the words of Craig Broyles:

---

[3]See Gerstenberger, *Psalms*, 36.

[4]See Ricoeur, *The Rule of Metaphor*, and Crossan, ed., *Paul Ricoeur and Biblical Hermeneutics*.

[5]Ricoeur, *Essays on Biblical Interpretation*, 1.

[6]See Ricoeur, *Interpretation Theory*, esp. 34-37, 92-95. On liturgy as a "world-making enterprise," see Brueggemann, *Israel's Praise*.

[7]See also Sallie McFague, *Speaking in Parables: A Study in Metaphor and Theology* (Philadelphia: Fortress, 1975) and *Metaphorical Theology: Models of God in Religious Language* (Philadelphia: Fortress, 1982) esp. 42. McFague also emphasizes that biblical God language is metaphorical in nature.

[8]Elizabeth Achtemeier, *The Old Testament and the Proclamation of the Gospel* (Philadelphia: Westminster Press, 1973) 42-44.

[9]See Bellinger, *Psalmody and Prophecy*, 60-61; *Psalms*, 144-45.

Such findings give us deeper insight into the faith represented in the Psalter. In these psalms we see Israel's faith in a position of extremity, when circumstances test that faith with challenge and lead to a critical examination of faith's foundation. In the psalms of plea when distress is encountered it is met with petition, which seeks to actualize expectations engendered by praise traditions. These psalms give no evidence that expectation has been disappointed. God is not accused of having had a role in the distress. Thus, for example, when enemies threaten, God is simply called upon as a third party to come to the rescue. That one (even if he be "righteous") may encounter distress and subsequently call on Yahweh appears to be a given in Israelite faith. This is confirmed by the conception of God as a refuge, so often seen in the Psalms. Yahweh is the Deliverer, which means that one may not presume that he is a guardian who preserves his own from even the sight of evil. His salvation is known by a series of saving acts, not by a continual state of salvation. He is the God of the heights who reaches down to the depths (cf. Ps. 113).[10]

Westermann's phrase is the God who delivers.[11] God is certainly present in the sanctuary, but the primary activity is response to the prayer for help. Perhaps the most appropriate image for our text is Walter Brueggemann's: the God who embraces pain.[12] What is God doing in Psalm 61? *God embraces pain* by embracing the one who is pained.

2. What does Psalm 61 tell us about prayer? We must infer a response, but the question is central. The Psalter could be called "Prayer Book of the Bible."[13] The first Psalm introduces the book in terms of instruction to be meditated upon constantly (v. 2), and the primary instruction relates to prayer, an activity central to the life of faith. Psalm 61 is a prayer; it addresses God (v. 2). Our investigation of the psalm's cultic setting indicated that the psalm is essentially a prayer for protection closely associated with the sanctuary. The fact that one in distress calls upon God gives focus to the general perspective of the lament psalms: one

---

[10]Broyles, *Conflict of Faith and Experience*, 222-23.

[11]Westermann, *What Does the Old Testament Say about God?* 25-38, and *Elements of Old Testament Theology*, 35ff.

[12]Walter Brueggemann, "A Shape for Old Testament Theology, II: Embrace of Pain," *CBQ* 47 (1985): 395-415.

[13]See Bellinger, *Psalms*, 1-7.

never moves beyond addressing God. No matter how close one comes to the overwhelming chaos of death, that circumstance still resides within the sphere of faith and spoken encounter with God. Petition infuses the whole of Psalm 61 (vv. 2-3, 5, 7-8).[14] In addition, v. 6 speaks of divine response and v. 9 of praise.

Psalm 61 implies that prayer is a dialogue between God and worshiper(s). This dialogue nurtures the life-giving relationship that is central to the psalm. I have characterized the relationship in terms of "I-Thou"; the speaker, from a setting of distress, addresses God. This dialogue is also quite honest. The Psalter is the example *par excellence* of the honest dialogue of faith. It offers praise, cries out for justice and deliverance, and seeks forgiveness. And Psalm 61, along with other psalms, affirms that God accepts such bold words. Psalm 61 also reminds us that lament is essential to faith and worship. Contemporary worship often leaves the impression that God is either distant and static, blessing complacency, or that God is so familiar as to be an admired chum. Worshiping communities today often miss the vibrancy of honest laments.[15] They make up a major proportion of biblical prayers.

Psalm 61 is a prayer, and we can learn from it about this significant aspect of faith. *Prayer is the honest dialogue of faith* springing from one's condition in life, whatever it may be. Such a perspective is endemic to Old Testament theology.

3. What is the relationship between individual and community? Ps 61:2-6 contains two petitions, one followed by motivation and the other by an affirmation of response. From that point, the scope of the prayer broadens beyond the individual to the community and its leader, the king. The king was to be the guarantor of justice for the whole people and, ideally, the righteous symbol of the community ancient Israel. The Old Testament gives a primary place to community. Although the individual comes to the fore, for example, in the individual lament psalms, it is always the individual as part of the community.

---

[14]See Tate, *Psalms 51-60*, 116.

[15]See Walter Brueggemann, "The Costly Loss of Lament," *JSOT* 36 (1986): 57-71; also note the comment of Fewell, "Feminist Reading of the Hebrew Bible," 77, that we read to be broadened, deepened, and transformed. The often unfamiliar lament psalms certainly provide such an opportunity.

Western intellectual history and theology have tended in recent times to assert the primacy of the individual. Worthy of note is the contrast that even an intense, individual prayer such as Psalm 61 concludes with an emphasis on community. Life and faith are not possible outside of community (note Psalm 133). Psalm 61 reflects *the centrality of community for faith.* Such a perspective challenges any "rugged individualism."

4. From one perspective, Psalm 61 is a prayer for protection. I have argued for a cultic setting in which the speaker seeks and receives the protection afforded "those who fear your name." All of the petitions seek protection: vv. 3, 5 for the speaker and vv. 7-8 for the king. The affirmation of God's past action in v. 4 characterizes God as refuge and protecting tower. Indeed most of the psalm pertains to "protection." Following v. 5 there is a shift from plea for divine protection to confidence in receiving it.

What is the psalm's theology of protection? First of all, the psalm is realistic. It recognizes the difficulties of life and the enemy and brings such realities to expression in the honest dialogue of faith. The protection it seeks is associated with the divine presence at the sanctuary. We have already noted the connections between sanctuary and asylum in the Old Testament. The sanctuary was the primary place of divine presence, which provided the essential blessing for wholeness of life. Here the community gathered for worship. Here they encountered hope for life and, as in Psalm 61, hoped-for protection in the face of crisis and oppression. It is significant to note that the shift from petition to confidence in the psalm has a basis in worship. That shift is crucial to the psalm's theological perspective, and the whole experience is in the context of worship. The psalm does not tell us how one moves from crisis to hope, from "the end of the earth" to "the shelter of your wings," but it does make clear that community worship is essential to the process.[16] In a world in which chaos knocks at the door, protection becomes a pressing

---

[16]From the perspective of the New Testament, one might say that the church as the body of Christ (faith community) assumes the function of making known the divine presence (sanctuary). Thus, one task of the worshiping community is to provide protection for the troubled and wronged. Throughout history many church buildings and communities have offered "sanctuary," protection, for the troubled and oppressed who seek just intervention.

issue. Psalm 61 offers no false, naive answer. It does, however, press us toward *the community at worship as the context for searching out genuine hope of protection.*

5. The psalm derives from a setting of crisis. What does it say about encounter with trouble? We have considered various alternatives for the crisis giving rise to the text. Verses 2-5 certainly reflect trouble—a cry for help, a fainting heart, the enemy, need for protection. The speaker clearly experiences pain.[17] Encounters with pain are inherent to a full life. What the psalm does is "theologize" the encounter with trouble, that is, process the experience in the context of faith. Broyles says the Psalms interpret the experience.[18] So the encounter with trouble is part of the life of faith. The denial of pain, trouble, and death is not an act of faith.[19] Rather, the issue is how one deals with the difficulty. Psalm 61 brings the issue to the community. That community is gathered in worship. In that context, the worshiper addresses God with the pain of life. God is one worthy of trust and praise, the God who delivers, the one present in Zion. The current crisis challenges faith. The psalm seeks to integrate faith and reality. The pain is real, and in the process of encountering the psalm, the community experiences also the reality of faith in God. Not all psalms take the same course, but the conclusion is hopeful in Psalm 61. Pain is part of the life of faith. *The psalm expresses the pain in order to help us move through it.*

Old Testament texts provide new ways of looking at life. We identify with those texts, and they liberate us to bring life to theological expression. They present new possibilities. Such is also the case with Psalm 61. What possibilities does it present? What "world" does it create? How can we summarize our theological reflections in Ricoeur's terms? Psalm 61 portrays a vibrant person fully involved in life and in the worshiping community. Faith provides the foundation for a full life. But this life is not one cluttered with piosity. It is a bold life eager to encounter what creation affords and holding God responsible for the promise of enabling

---

[17]See Bellinger, *Psalms*, 139-40.

[18]Broyles, *Conflict of Faith and Experience.*

[19]See Brueggemann, "Shape for Old Testament Theology"; "Formfulness of Grief," *Int* 31 (1977): 263-75; and "From Hurt to Joy, From Death to Life," *Int* 28 (1974): 3-19.

presence. The dialogue of faith offers renewal in the midst of life. Pain is real in this life and becomes a part of the dialogue. God embraces the pain and thereby offers hope.

Ancient Israel went into Egypt seeking food for life. In time, they were oppressed and enslaved. Their groan was heard, and God embraced their pain (Exod 3:7-10). God brought them out to a new orientation, a new way of living as the community of faith and worship.[20] Through the experience of pain came newness, but the pain leaves a mark of realism; simplistic answers no longer suffice. Only a bold faith can now lead them forward. This "root metaphor" of ancient Israel rings true to our psalm.

Our description of the "world" of Psalm 61 has thus far been rather abstract, as is the whole notion of theological meaning we have been considering. Western theology and intellectual history have been dominated by an idealist view of the world in which the articulation of meaning is primary. Certainly meaning, theology, and thought have a crucial role in developing lifestyle; but the interaction between thought and action is far more complex than we often assume in a one-dimensional movement from thought to action. The Biblical revelation tends to be quite life-centered and to place primary emphasis on living our days in faith and justice. The goal is the transformation of life. In this sense, the function of a text for a community's life moves to the heart of the matter. My point is that when we have begun to live a life of honest and bold prayer and faith in community, of participating in providing sanctuary for the troubled and oppressed, then we will far more fully understand the import of a text like Psalm 61.

Conclusion

Our final look at Psalm 61 has raised questions from an explicitly theological point of view. I have suggested that the "world" which the psalm opens up is one in which the life of faith realistically faces pain

---

[20]See Walter Brueggemann, "Psalms and the Life of Faith: A Suggested Typology of Function," *JSOT* 17 (1980): 3-32. See also, on the Exodus passage, Westermann, *What Does the Old Testament Say about God?* 30-32; and *Elements of Old Testament Theology*, 35ff. The call of Moses to lead the people out of Egypt brings to mind the part of the community in effecting liberation from trouble and injustice.

and addresses it to God who embraces pain. In the context of the worshiping community, it is possible to encounter sanctuary as a means to moving forward in the pilgrimage of faith. The intensity of the psalm calls hearers/readers to living and facilitating such a lifestyle.

This final reflection on Psalm 61, a theological reflection, leads us back to the issues with which our study began, hermeneutical issues. We must now reflect again on our pilgrimage with the psalm and on the implications of the methodological approach used thus far. The concluding section of the volume will do that and will seek to respond to objections which might arise because of the book's approach.

Afterword

Summary

This study began with an attempt to articulate a hermeneutical framework as a starting point for our treatment of Psalm 61. The hermeneutic of curiosity I proposed took into account the current debate in biblical studies over the nature of interpretation and the history of interpretation. Growing out of a challenge to pre-Enlightenment approaches, the historical-critical approach came to dominate biblical studies in this century. Historical criticism has now been challenged by various New Critical, structuralist, and poststructuralist works. Variety in approach now characterizes biblical interpretation.

Questions of origin, study of the shape of the text itself, and attention to the reader are all part of the web of interpretation. Historical-critical methods such as source, form, and redaction criticism deal with questions of origin. More "text-immanent" studies call on poetic, structural and rhetorical analyses, while reader-response criticism gives focus to interpretive communities. This plurality of methods is basic to a hermeneutic of curiosity which explores matters of origin, text, and reader. All these matters contribute to our explorations of texts. Such explorations issue in multiple readings of texts; to ignore aspects of this web of interpretation is to miss helpful dimensions of interpretation. This volume has tested this hermeneutic of curiosity and methodological pluralism on Psalm 61.

The appendix contains a close look at the text as a prayer for help; even there the ambiguity of the poem comes to the fore because several of the psalm's verbs could be translated as statements of confidence as well as petitions. Form-critical matters of genre and setting occupied our attention in chapters 1 and 2. Again, several ways to explore the form of the psalm are plausible, but I have given special attention to one view. I have read Psalm 61 as an individual lament with three sections. Verses 2-4 are petition followed by motivation; vv. 5-6 extend the plea; and v.

6 reflects assurance of God's response. Verses 7-9 extend the prayer further with a petition for the king followed by a vow of praise; thus they
give the psalm a positive conclusion. Chapter 2 considered various
proposals for the setting from which the psalm arose. Again, "assured results" are not possible in such a reconstructive exploration, but I
proposed a setting related to protection associated with the sanctuary. The
cult supports the cry to move from the power of death and oppression to
the hope of life and justice. Our look at the canonical context of Psalm
61 has reminded us that the psalm is in a literary context in the Psalter
and that it has found broader application beyond the Jerusalem cult. This
application began in the postexilic era and has continued in faith communities for centuries.

Awareness of the canonical shape of the psalm leads readers to consider the "text itself." We explored various literary dimensions of the text
and found a poetic form with a dynamic unfolding of movement from
crisis to hope. The poem moves through its sections in a structure of
intensification from petition to hope. Chapter 5 considered the place of
the reader in interpretation. We looked at the process of reading and
issues which arise from the reader's context. Some of those issues are
theological in character.

Our probings of Psalm 61 have revealed a petition, an individual
lament structured in typical ways, a prayer for temple protection, a prayer
for the protection of a dispersed community of faith, a persuasive poem
which affirms God's protection and nurtures faith, and a poem in dialogue with readers' concerns about faith and divine action in the world.
I have generated multiple readings of the text. The methodological pluralism has issued in a variety of nuances for the interpretation of the text.
This work has been something of an experimental model, and the various
approaches have provided different views of the psalm, all of which are
helpful in attempting to read it fully.

Remaining Questions

*Some readers of this volume may respond that the approach is too
eclectic.* The approach is in a sense eclectic, but I would prefer to describe it as pluralistic. It is not indecisive. I have argued for various posi-
tions in treating the text and sought to make critical judgments. I would
insist that a methodological pluralism which considers various aspects of
interpretation—origin, text, reader—is endemic to our historical moment.

But one might also respond that the approach is idealistic. I understand that reader-response critics are not suddenly going to commit their lives to the task of form criticism and *vice versa*. At the same time, it is a mistake for any interpreter to ignore help from any source. Form-critical analysis may provide help to a canonical critic or a reader-response critic. Reader-oriented criticism may help the rhetorical critic or the form critic. At the base of my argument is the assertion that no reading of a text is complete, including this volume's readings of Psalm 61. Various approaches provide help in the interpretive task. As readers pursue their own approach, they can at least be open to help from different approaches. Interdisciplinary or cooperative efforts hold promise.

Our work suffers when we cut ourselves off from potential help, even though the assumptions of other methods may differ. Historical-critical, text-immanent, and reader-oriented paradigms differ, but an interpreter can enter a paradigm and explore a text on that basis. I have freely admitted that the notion of historical objectivity is an illusion, but we can summon enough objectivity to use a method to gain any help it affords. I am suggesting a "metaparadigm" of methodological pluralism which is at the heart of a hermeneutic of curiosity. To ignore historical-critical concerns would constitute a "monumental failure of nerve," and to reject newer literary and reader-oriented methodologies would constitute a fundamentalist attitude which is counterproductive to scholarship and the hermeneutical task. Probings of texts from any conceivable angle are the essence of literary method. We need—and can get—help from various directions. Essential to this first starting point is the assumption that an interpreter read in sympathy with the text at hand and then come to critical judgments in the process of interpretation.

Some may also respond that my approach is elitist. Only a professional biblical scholar can spend so much time on a brief psalm, much less deal with the myriad of questions related to hermeneutics and methods. The approach appears designed for ivory-tower scholars who have the luxury of time to cogitate over such obscure issues. In a sense, the approach is elitist and intentionally so. I am addressing an academic audience whose task is to engage in scholarship. The profession rightly insists on the best use of skills and that at the highest level attainable.

In another sense, however, the approach is not elitist. Every reader of Psalm 61—whether professional biblical scholar, member of a local congregation, or one who approaches the text out of literary interests—considers the matters treated in this study. The psalm's words, their relationships, the historical background, the history of the text's appropriation, the use of language, how readers make sense of the poem—all of those issues are involved when a person reads Psalm 61, even if at an elementary level. The task is to become better readers and thus to pool information helpful to the task. Professional scholars are in a place to provide constructive leadership for the practice of interpretation at various levels.

The very proposal of a hermeneutic of curiosity suggests an inclusive approach. All questions from all readers are fair game. In the process of dealing with questions, readers make critical judgments as they can. Scholarship can inform those judgments, but my hermeneutical model supports the inclusion of questions from any reader.

That statement leads to another question. *Some readers may well be concerned about the issue of validity in interpretation.* E. D. Hirsch has raised the issue most forcefully.[1] The concern is about the multivalence of texts; they express multiple meanings. Hirsch seeks to limit meaning to authorial intent. I have suggested that multivalence is more realistic, but that assertion raises a serious question: Are there any limits to appropriate interpretation? Can a text mean anything? Can we determine meaning? Is chaos the rule of the day? Is there no order in the pluralism of contemporary hermeneutical approaches such as I have proposed?

I should first say that the question is primarily one deriving from the concerns of white males because the attempt to limit a passage to one meaning can easily degenerate into the attempt to control. There is a social basis for the question; it comes from the dominant western culture of which I am a part. At the same time, the question also has a scholarly basis. I celebrate the multivalence of texts, the diversity which is now part of the practice of hermeneutics. But if all interpretations are equal, chaos does indeed reign. If there are no limits to interpretation, "meaning" may even become a meaningless category. To affirm multivalence does not affirm that "anything goes in interpretation."

An additional aspect of the question arises for some biblical scholars, the question of biblical authority. Communities of faith read the Bible as canon, as rule or authority for life and faith. How can a text be authorita-

---

[1] Hirsch, *Validity in Interpretation* and *The Aims of Interpretation*.

tive if there are no limits to its interpretation? I read Psalm 61 as a sacred text, a part of Scripture. That confession accentuates the question of validity in interpretation.

Now let me speak to the question. First, I am not arguing that the meaning of a text is indeterminate or that one proposal for a text's meaning is as good as another. I have not followed the route of deconstruction. Our knowledge is limited, but I have already indicated that I find the path of deconstruction asks too high a price. The result is a continuing array of possibilities which leads to no end. That view fails to reckon with the fact that people make critical judgments about texts and live based upon them. The existential relation between text and reader clearly assumes social settings and conventions, but those presuppositions are foundational for readers. Deconstruction itself finally deconstructs on its endless path when it sees texts and readers meaningfully related. To argue for multivalence is not to argue that one reading of a text is as good as another.

Rather, I would argue that the text is meaningful, that is, full of meaning. We seldom, if ever, reach the depths and richness which a text holds. All our readings are incomplete; to think otherwise would be the epitomy of arrogance. I have given up the attempt to craft some definitive, integrated interpretation of Psalm 61. The text is too vibrant for that. I do not mean that "anything goes," but realizing the multivalence of the text liberates me to explore various aspects of the psalm.

Second, when I interpret a text, I make my case and the hearing/reading community judges whether it accepts my findings. At one level, then, the community evaluates my interpretation. The various interpretive communities of which I partake—scholarly, theological, and social, among others—influence my interpretations and judge their value.[2] That is helpful to the question of validity in interpretation, but does not solve the problem. Different communities evaluate interpretations in different ways. How can one adjudicate between communities? The difficulty persists.

Third, let me suggest one way forward with the question. I have proposed a hermeneutic in which questions of origin, text, and reader all come into play. I repeat the diagram from the introductory chapter.

---

[2]See Fish, *Is There a Text in This Class?*

TEXT

ORIGIN   READER

Each approach, from origin, text, or reader, provides an angle of vision in the interpretive process. However, note that the text is the point of departure. The text leads to questions of origin and is the window into that history. The text has a shape of its own. It is the text which leads us to readers and the reading process. The text is at the center of the hermeneutical task; without it, no interpretation takes place. It is the basis of our work and it is the constant throughout the process. The text's origin, its rhetoric, and its beckoning to readers are all rolled into the text we now have. When we debate interpretations, it is the text to which we appeal; textual support provides the basis for evaluating readings. So perhaps the text sets some bounds for us.

Paul Ricoeur has eloquently spoken of texts taking on a life of their own, and yet he also speaks of the meaning of texts in the worlds they project.[3] Various readings speak to dimensions of those worlds. Meir Sternberg certainly is an eminent reader-response critic, but he also speaks of the text leading the reader with clues to proper interpretation.[4] Edgar McKnight has also argued for a reader-oriented criticism in which the reader is led by structures and codes in the text.[5] While we may not be able to speak of a single meaning of a text determined by authorial or historical intent, we can speak of literary intent. Reading is the production of meaning and the locus of that meaning is in an interaction between text and reader. The web of interpretation commends various paths for readers to appropriate. Yet, one is reading a particular text which gives direction for the task. Texts do support boundaries for interpretation. Those boundaries are in the context of the goal of interpretation.

Let me illustrate. When, in his 1938 commentary, Moses Buttenwieser read Psalm 61, he suggested that the text derived from the years

---

[3]Ricoeur, *Interpretation Theory*, 79, 92-95; see also Iser, *The Act of Reading*, esp. 20, 38, 118.

[4]Sternberg, *Poetics of Biblical Narrative*, 7-23, 41-57.

[5]McKnight, *Postmodern Use of the Bible.*

318–312 B.C.E. and reflected the difficulties of those years following the death of Alexander the Great.[6] He eliminates vv. 7-8, with the reference to the king, from consideration because he asserts that these verses originally belonged to Psalm 72. Thus he can assign a late date to Psalm 61. Buttenwieser seeks the psalm's historical meaning, but there is little in the text to support his conclusions. The removal of vv. 7-8 is arbitrary. While Buttenwieser does point to other psalms he says come from a similar time, it is fair to say that there is nothing in the text to support his particular historical placement of Psalm 61. As a historical reading, his interpretation fails because of the lack of textual support.

Another possibility would be a messianic interpretation of the psalm. That reading is plausible if we accept certain assumptions, as one reader response; but if the goal was to convey the psalm's initial referent, the text offers little support. There is no reference to Messiah. The king was naturally the Davidic king in Jerusalem. If the interpretive goal is a historical one, a messianic reading does not fare well, and the basis of that evaluation is the textual evidence.

Consider a more contemporary illustration. Undergraduate students I have taught might well interpret the psalm something like the following: Psalm 61 simply says it's neat that God is going to take care of us. The text of our psalm does speak of God's protection, but this interpretation ignores the fact that the protection comes in the midst of genuine difficulty, not to speak of the fact that the Book of Psalms in which Psalm 61 occurs fully embraces the pain of life and understands God to be involved with pain and not with avoiding it. This optimistic contemporary interpretation will not stand up to the basic literary pattern of the psalm. Our text is a prayer in the midst of crisis and affirms God's positive response. That basic literary intent provides some parameters for our reading. I have evaluated this last interpretation by inquiring into its textual basis.[7]

These illustrations are basic ones, but perhaps they demonstrate the point that texts do provide help in evaluating interpretations. What I have said has in no way dealt satisfactorily with the issue of validity in inter-

---

[6]Buttenwieser, *Psalms Chronologically Treated*, 756-58.

[7]My comments also suggest the importance of dealing with texts' genre in evaluating interpretation.

pretation. Texts generate multiple readings. Meaning is not indeterminate, but there are various possibilities. The response of interpretive communities offers some help as does the basic sense of the text. The plain sense of the text provides guidance.[8] However, the appropriate parameters, or the way to those parameters, of interpretation in our current pluralistic setting still have not become clear.[9]

Mary Ann Tolbert provides a helpful list of criteria for adjudicating interpretations:

> 1. An interpretation of a text should be in accord with the standards of intellectual discourse of its day. . . .

---

[8]See Mieke Bal, *Death & Dissymmetry: The Politics of Coherence in the Book of Judges*, Chicago Studies in the History of Judaism (Chicago/London: University of Chicago Press, 1988) 238-41. Consider her formulation on 240:

> The text is not an object upon which we can operate; it is another subject that speaks to us. We can listen, and just as in real life, we will hear our own voice reflected; yet we cannot attribute just anything to the other speaker. If we shout too loud, so that the other is reduced to silence, we will lack arguments to make our case. This is the point of rational argumentation, of the attempt to give evidence in the text while we do not believe interpretations can ever be truly based on it. It is not a matter of empirical proof; it is a matter of plausible interaction.
>
> If my readers have not been able to hear the voice of the text resound in my interpretations, I have simply missed my goal and will not be believed. Hence, there is a third party in the dialogue, the witness who checks what happens and who will refuse to go along when the interpreter overwrites the text.

Also worthy of note is Bal's statement in "Dealing/With/Women: Daughters in the Book of Judges," *The Book and the Text*, 16, and Iser's description of meaning as something that happens (*The Act of Reading*, 22). Susan Marie Praeder, "Jesus-Paul, Peter-Paul, and Jesus-Peter Parallelisms in Luke-Acts: A History of Reader-Response," SBLSP 23 (1984): 38-39, cautions against "the temptation to make sense of the text" and the temptation for the all-powerful reader to run roughshod over the text.

[9]David C. Steinmetz, "The Superiority of Pre-Critical Exegesis," *Theology Today* 37 (1980): 27-38, draws interesting parallels between our contemporary hermeneutical context and precritical interpretation. His suggestion of "a field of possible meanings" is helpful, but how one defines the field is still unclear.

2. The more fully an interpretation can demonstrate its points from the text itself, the more convincing it becomes. . . .
3. The more coherence an interpretation can disclose in a text, the more persuasive it becomes. . . .
4. An interpretation should be cognizant of the general historical, literary, and sociological matrix out of which the text comes. . . .
5. An interpretation should be illuminating and interesting.[10]

I suspect that she is more optimistic than I about our success in evaluating interpretations, but her view reflects something of my argument. The phenomena of the text give bases for evaluation, and one needs to be aware of social location. Awareness of the text's social location may help the interpreter consider her/his own social location (interpretive community). Essential to the process of interpretation is dialogue among various interpretive communities. "Dialogue" may be more realistic than "adjudication"; and when dialogue occurs, perhaps the question of validity in interpretation does become less significant.[11]

Some readers of this volume may have an additional remaining question. *They may wish to challenge my choice of methods for reading Psalm 61.* If I am genuinely interested in a methodological pluralism, why not also make use of the methods popular in the pre-Enlightenment era? I have used historical-critical tools; why not precritical? In a sense I have done so, for much precritical interpretation was a kind of reader response to the text. Allegory often related the text to the context of the interpreter or reader. That is not to say that reader-oriented criticism is precritical; the era is different. But there is a reader-oriented element to much precritical interpretation. At the same time, I am a child of the Enlightenment; I cannot deny that and do not wish to do so. The Enlightenment and the historical-critical approach have had a lasting impact on our world. We cannot go back to the precritical consensus. We rather move

---

[10]Mary Ann Tolbert, *Sowing the Seed: Mark's World in Literary-Historical Perspective* (Minneapolis: Fortress Press, 1989) 10-13.

[11]See Jeffrey Stout, "What Is the Meaning of a Text?" *New Literary History* 14 (1982): 1-12; Stephen Fowl, "The Ethics of Interpretation or What's Left Over after the Elimination of Meaning," SBLSP 27 (1988): 69-81; Gary A. Phillips, "Exegesis as Critical Praxis: Reclaiming History and Text from a Postmodern Perspective," *Poststructural Criticism and the Bible: Text/History/Discourse, Semeia* 51 (Atlanta: Scholars Press, 1990): 7-49.

forward to a post-Enlightenment or poststructuralist age in which historical-critical methods can, within acknowledged limits, play a part. So a hermeneutic of curiosity is inclusive, though we simply do not live in a pre-Enlightenment age.

Some may also question the fact that I have, in a sense, followed the history of scholarship by dealing with form and canonical criticism as historical approaches and then considered text-immanent exegesis and reader-response criticism. I have followed that sequence, in part, as a reflection of my pilgrimage through the hermeneutical issues. Would the volume look different if I had begun with reader response or with a rhetorical analysis? Perhaps the tone would be different, but the use of each method is still appropriate and I suspect would bring similar, if not the same, results.

Perhaps a more significant issue is the fact that three chapters concern aspects of origin and only one each has to do with text and with reader. That reflects the dominance of the historical-critical approach in this century and in contemporary biblical studies. In time, we may have as much material on text-immanent approaches to psalms or on reader-oriented probings of poetic texts, but we do not now. My use of methods has thus reflected contemporary practice, though I hope it also moves us forward if only by a step. When I have used historical-critical tools, I have done so in a context rather different than that in which the historical-critical approach dominated for most of the last two centuries. I have put form criticism in a more pluralistic framework.

Finally, some may wonder about concluding with theological issues. Does that influence the use of diverse methods? Again, I would argue that the use of each method will stand on its own. Chapter six has also made the case for a textual basis for a theological approach to the psalm.

Thus my choice of methods may raise questions, and it is not the only path to follow; it is one of the legitimate ways to enter the web of hermeneutical issues.

Conclusion

I have spoken to some of the remaining questions. Let me conclude by repeating some of the significant aspects of this experiment.

We live in a world characterized by pluralism. That is true in the hermeneutical sphere and in terms of methods used in biblical studies. It is also true in the broader world of ideologies which compete for the loyalty of people and communities. This volume has argued for a pluralistic approach to biblical interpretation through a hermeneutic of curiosity. That option corresponds well with the shape of contemporary life, and the volume has demonstrated the value of the enterprise in relation to a representative text, Psalm 61.

We have closely examined Psalm 61. That is a contribution. Beyond that and the hermeneutical framework, the consideration of canonical, rhetorical, and reader-response tools for studying the text moves us forward. I have attempted to explore the various dimensions of the interpretive task with the psalm. And yet it is inevitable that the interpretive task is never complete. All readings are incomplete. They may contribute significantly but still be incomplete. Additional readings often bring different, enlightening angles of vision. There is much left to do. That is so with literature, and particularly so with biblical literature. The task continues with dynamism.

Craig Broyles has emphasized that the task of the scholar is to enable others to better read a text.[12] The task is to send the reader back to the text with a more constructive orientation, to enable the text to speak. This volume has pursued that task in its various aspects.

Human curiosity abounds. It leads to many constructive discoveries and has much yet to offer. That curiosity will continue to lead us to probe the depths of biblical texts.

---

[12]Broyles, *The Conflict of Faith and Experience*, 33-34.

Appendix
Translation and Comment

Introduction

The basis of our study is the Hebrew text of Psalm 61. Most contemporary readers, however, will not know Hebrew and thus translation becomes important. The very fact that the text is in Hebrew invites the contemporary reader to translate into a modern language. A translation attempts to communicate a text and in that sense also is integral to the task of interpretation. Various parts of this study have an impact on translations, but readers also need to keep the translation in mind as a basis for the study. I also include comments on textual and exegetical issues.

Translation

[1]To the choirmaster.   Upon stringed instruments.   Of David.
[2]Hear, O God, my cry;
      attend to my prayer.
[3]From the end of the earth I call unto you when my heart is faint;
      lead me to a rock high beyond me,
[4]for you have been a refuge for me,
      a strong tower in the face of the enemy.
[5]Let me sojourn in your tent always;
      let me take refuge in the shelter of your wings.   Selah.
[6]Indeed, you, O God, have heard my vows;
      you have given the heritage of those who fear your name.
[7]Add days upon days for the king,
      his years as generation after generation.
[8]May he be enthroned forever before God;
      appoint loyalty and trustworthiness that they may preserve him.
[9]Thus I will praise your name forever
      as I fulfil my vows day by day.

Comment

Verse 1. עַל־נְגִינַת indicates accompaniment upon stringed instruments. The translation reflects the fact that a number of manuscripts and
versions indicate the plural here, a reading that does not change the con-
sonantal text.[1] The form most commonly found in the Psalms superscriptions is בִּנְגִינֹת (Pss. 4:1; 6:1; 54:1; 67:1; 76:1). However, the reading
in the Massoretic Text could stand as the form with the old feminine
ending rather than as a noun in the construct state.[2] לְדָוִד is the shorter
way the psalm superscriptions indicate a Davidic psalm.[3]

Verse 2. Vaticanus[4] leaves out אֱלֹהִים, but that fact does not provide
sufficient warrant for omitting it from the translation. The psalm is part
of the Elohistic Psalter, and thus the use of this divine name is to be expected. The imperatives in the verse reflect a sense of urgency in the
prayer. Both terms describing the prayer, רִנָּתִי and תְּפִלָּתִי reflect a
cultic background but are rather general in nature.[5] רִנָּתִי indicates a
prayer of entreaty, a ringing cry for help.

Verse 3. The second line of this verse provides the most interesting
textual issue in the psalm. It reads literally, "To a rock (which is) high
from me (you) lead me." The use of the preposition מִמֶּנִּי indicates the
comparative degree, from which derives the popular English translation,
"Lead me to the rock that is higher than I" (NRSV). A more likely view is
that the preposition suggests that the rock of safety is high away from the
speaker, out of reach.[6] The speaker needs assistance to reach this rock.
Such an understanding of the line accepts the text as it stands. That
appears to be the best option, though the Septuagint seems to construe

---

[1]See *BHS*.

[2]See GKC §80f.

[3]Mowinckel offers an interpretation of לַמְנַצֵּחַ rather different from that of
our translation (*The Psalms in Israel's Worship*, 2:212-13).

[4]See *BHS*.

[5]See E. Gerstenberger, "פלל," *TWAT* 6, cols. 609, 611; Ficker, "רנן," *THAT*
2, cols. 782-85; J. F. A. Sawyer, "Types of Prayer in the Old Testament," *Semitics* 7 (1980): 131-43; K. Heinen, "Das Nomen tᵉfilla als Gattungsbezeichnung,"
BZ 17 (1973): 103-105; N. E. Wagner, "*Rinnah* in the Psalter," *VT* 10 (1960):
435-41.

[6]See GKC, §133c.

יְרוֹם מִמֶּנִּי as the *polel* of the verb, "lift me up." The Greek and Syriac translators apparently understood the line as an expression of faith: "You lifted me up to a rock; you comforted me."[7] The verse appears to be an expansion of the plea begun in v. 1, and so I have rendered the Massoretic Text as a petition.[8]

Verse 3 also provides a significant case of poetic ambiguity. The New Revised Standard Version and the *Revised Psalter* divide the verse and connect the first line with v. 2 and the second line with v. 4. In addition, the translator could construe בַּעֲטֹף לְבִּי as part of the second line of the verse: "When I (my courage and will) faint within, lead me. . . ." The Hebrew certainly allows such translations, if we ignore the Massoretic accentuation; but the link between crying out and fainting is natural in the Psalms (note, for example, the superscription to Psalm 102). The comments on the form of the Psalm in chapter one also suggest that we read vv. 2-4 together.

Verse 4. The causal particle כִּי introduces the motivation that God has in the past provided protection. The request is that God do so again (see Pss. 10:14; 27:9; 59:17; 63:8). The perfect הָיִיתָ could also refer to God's habitual action, suggesting a present tense translation, "you are my refuge."[9] On this reading, the verse describes God as the one who provides strong protection from the presence of (against) the enemy, and thus the prayer for help comes to אֱלֹהִים. אוֹיֵב could be taken as a collective, "enemies."

Verse 5. Our translation takes the verse as a continuation of the petition; the cohortative אָגוּרָה makes a request,[10] and the plural form עוֹלָמִים provides further intensity.[11] The introductory cry for help (v. 2) provides the contextual clue that the psalm is a petition. At the same time, it is possible to translate the verbs of this verse as statements of

---

[7]See *BHS*. The last verb in the Syriac translation presumably reflects the root נחם rather than נחה.

[8]See Diethelm Michel, *Tempora und Satzstellung in den Psalmen*, Abhandlungen zur Evangelischer Theologie 1 (Bonn: H. Bouvier u. Co. Verlag, 1960) 82, 150, 218.

[9]See ibid., 88.

[10]Ibid., 153.

[11]BDB, 762; E. Jenni, "עוֹלָם," *THAT* 2, col. 230.

confidence: "I will sojourn in your tent always; I will take refuge under the shelter of your wings."[12]

In vv. 3-5, we encounter ambiguity in the verbs.[13] The same will be true in vv. 7-8. I have taken the introductory plea of v. 2 as the contextual clue for translating the psalm as a petition. However, the verbs of vv. 3, 5, 7, 8 may also be translated as indicative statements of confidence. It is not that the ambiguity is intentional so much as it is that our attempts to translate the Hebrew text into English simply bear both possibilities. The decision one makes influences the direction of further studies on the psalm. The case for translating vv. 3, 5, 7, 8 as petitions is strong, but we need to keep the other possibility in mind.[14]

Verse 6. The particle כִּי introduces the statement with emphasis.[15] The preposition on לְנִדְרִי is unusual but is probably one of the places where ל is used with the direct object.[16] The translation of the second half of the verse follows the Massoretic Text, but many commentators emend יְרֻשַּׁת to אֶרֶשֶׁת, "desire" or "wish" in line with Ps. 21:3.[17] The bases for the change are the content and rather cryptic syntax. יְרֻשַּׁת usually indicates "possession, inheritance, heritage," with reference to land (see Deut. 2:5, 9, 19; Josh. 12:6,7; Judges 21:17).[18] Does the line mean "you have given (me) the heritage of those who fear your name?"

---

[12]However, note the comments of Gamberoni, "חסה," *TDOT* 5:67, 73, 75.

[13]On the notion of ambiguity, see Patrick D. Miller, "Poetic Ambiguity and Balance in Psalm XV," *VT* 39 (1979): 416-24; M. H. Abrams, *A Glossary of Literary Terms* (New York: Holt, Rinehart and Winston, 1971) 8-10.

[14]The issue comes to focus when one compares the translations of the Revised Standard Version, the New English Bible, the *Revised Psalter*, the *Jerusalem Bible*, and *The Psalms: A New Translation for Worship*. Most of the commentators seem to read the psalm in terms of petition, though note the comments of Eaton, *Psalms*, 157.

[15]See BDB, 472.

[16]See BDB, 511.

[17]See *BHS*; Anderson, *The Book of Psalms*, 1:449; Kraus, *Psalms 60-150*, 8; Gunkel, *Die Psalmen*, 260-61; Edward J. Kissane, *The Book of the Psalms*, vol. 1 (Dublin: Browne and Nolan Limited, 1953) 203; Oesterley, *Psalms*, 300.

[18]See, however, D. Winton Thomas, *The Text of the Revised Psalter* (London: SPCK, 1963) 23; and Dahood, *Psalms 2:86*, who suggest translating יְרֻשָּׁה as "desire, request."

Or does it mean "you have given those who fear your name (their) heritage?" Our study contains further comment.

Verse 7. The translation above takes this verse as a petition for the king by understanding תּוֹסִיף as an imperfect used in a jussive sense.[19] The verse seems to be a prayer that the reigning monarch (and dynasty) live long, that his years endure for generations, literally "(a) generation and (a) generation." A number of commentators read כִּימֵי for כְּמוֹ, "his years like the days from generation to generation."[20] The change, however, seems to make little difference to the overall sense of this rather idiomatic prayer. We have already noted the possibility of translating the verse as a statement of confidence rather than as a petition.[21]

Verse 8. יֵשֵׁב carries the sense of being seated on the throne.[22] In the second half of the verse, two manuscripts as well as Greek and Latin recensions omit the מַן.[23] The verb does seem a bit awkward here, but it is a shortened form of the *piel* imperative and gives good sense as "appoint, prepare."[24] An initial reading might suggest that the presence or absence of the form makes little difference to the overall sense of the verse. However, the imperative makes God's involvement more explicit and makes it difficult to read the verse as anything but a petition.[25] Our translation has followed that course. If one omits the imperative, this verse also could be either petition or statement of confidence. The retention of the נ in יִנְצְרֻהוּ relates to the fact that the verb is a pausal form.[26]

Verse 9. The closing verse opens with כֵּן, "so, thus." The cohortative אֲזַמְּרָה could indicate emphasis or a kind of petition, "let me

---

[19]GKC, §107n. See L. H. Brockington, *The Hebrew Text of the Old Testament* (Oxford: University Press, 1973) 135.

[20]See, e.g., *BHS* and Weiser, *Psalms*, 442; Gunkel, *Die Psalmen*, 260, 262.

[21]Michel, *Tempora und Satzstellung*, 169.

[22]BDB, 442.

[23]See *BHS*; Anderson, *Psalms*, 1:450; Kissane, *Psalms*, 1:203; A. A. Macintosh, *The Psalms: A New Translation for Worship. Notes on the Text* (London: Collins Liturgical Publications, 1977) 25. How would the form have made its way into the text? The suggestion of dittography carries little weight.

[24]GKC, §75cc.

[25]See Michel, *Tempora und Satzstellung*, 165.

[26]GKC, §66f.

praise."[27] The infinitive לְשַׁלְּמִי with preposition and suffix indicates purpose or aim: "while I pay my vows daily." יוֹם יוֹם carries the sense of "day after day."

Conclusion

This discussion of the text of Psalm 61 provides a basis for our study. Further comment is in the chapters pursuing various avenues of approach to the psalm. This brief look at the Hebrew text has revealed a prayer for help. At the same time, we have seen that one might also translate several of the psalm's verbs in terms of indicative statements of confidence rather than as petitions. The ambiguity present in the poem comes further to the fore in the remainder of the study.

---

[27]See Barth, "זמר," *TDOT* 4:93; Michel, *Tempora und Satzstellung*, 153.

Bibliography

Abrams, M. H. *A Glossary of Literary Terms*. New York: Holt, Rinehart, and Winston, 1971.

Achtemeier, Elizabeth. *The Old Testament and the Proclamation of the Gospel*. Philadelphia: Westminster Press, 1973.

Albertz, Rainer. *Persönliche Frömmigkeit und offizielle Religion*. CThM 9. Stuttgart: Calwer Verlag, 1978.

Albright, William Foxwell. *Yahweh and the Gods of Canaan*. New York: Doubleday, 1969.

Alter, Robert. *The Art of Biblical Poetry*. New York: Basic Books, 1985.

_____. "A Literary Approach to the Bible." *Commentary* 60 (1975): 70-77.

_____. "Psalms," in *The Literary Guide to the Bible*, ed. Robert Alter and Frank Kermode, 251-55. Cambridge MA: Harvard University Press, 1987.

Anderson, A. A. *The Book of Psalms*. Volume 1. NCB. London: Oliphants, 1972.

Auffret, Pierre. "'ALORS JE JOURERAI SANS FIN POUR TON NOM' Etude structurelle du psaume 61." *Science et Esprit* 36 (1984): 169-77.

_____. "Essai sur la structure literaire de Psaume 61." *JANES* 14 (1982): 1-10.

Bal, Mieke. "Dealing with Women: Daughters in the Book of Judges," in *The Book and the Text. The Bible and Literary Theory*, ed. Regina M. Schwartz, 16-39. Oxford: Basil Blackwell, 1990.

_____. *Death & Dissymmetry: The Politics of Coherence in the Book of Judges*. Chicago Studies in the History of Judaism. Chicago/London: University of Chicago Press, 1988.

Barnes, W. E. *The Psalms*. WC. London: Methuen & Co., 1931.

Barr, James. *The Bible in the Modern World*. London: SCM Press, 1973.

_____. "Childs's Introduction to the Old Testament as Scripture." *JSOT* 16 (1980): 12-23.

_____. *Holy Scripture: Canon, Authority, Criticism*. Oxford: Clarendon Press, 1983.

_____. "Reading the Bible as Literature." *BJRL* 56 (1973): 10-33.

Barré, Lloyd M. "The Riddle of the Flood Chronology." *JSOT* 41 (1988): 3-20.

Barth, C. "זמר." In *Theological Dictionary of the Old Testament*, ed. G. Johannes Botterweck and Helmer Ringgren, trans. David E. Green, 4:91-98. Grand Rapids MI: Eerdmans, 1980.

Barthes, Rolande. "The Death of the Author." In *Image—Music—Text*, ed. and trans. Stephen Heath, 142-48. New York: Hill & Wang, 1977.

Barton, John. "Classifying Biblical Criticism." *JSOT* 29 (1984): 19-35.

_____. *Reading the Old Testament: Method in Biblical Study*. Philadelphia: Westminster, 1984.

Becker, Joachim. *Israel Deutet seine Psalmen: Urformen und Neuinterpretation in den Psalmen*. SBS 18. Stuttgart: Katholisches Bibelwerk, 1966.

Beckson, K., and A. Ganz. *A Reader's Guide to Literary Terms: A Dictionary*. New York: Farrar, Straus, & Giroux, 1960.

Bellinger, W. H., Jr. *Psalmody and Prophecy*. JSOTSup 27. Sheffield: JSOT Press, 1984.

_____. *Psalms: Reading and Studying the Book of Praises*. Peabody MA: Hendrickson Publishers, 1990.

_____. "The Psalms and Acts: Reading and Rereading." In *With Steadfast Purpose: Essays on Acts in Honor of Henry Jackson Flanders, Jr.*, ed. Naymond H. Keathley, 127-43. Waco TX: Baylor University, 1990.

_____. "Psalm 26: A Test of Method." *VT* 43 (1993): 452-61.

Bentzen, Aage. *King and Messiah*. LSCB. London: Lutterworth, 1955.

Berlin, Adele. *The Dynamics of Biblical Parallelism*. Bloomington: Indiana University, 1985.

Berman, Art. *From the New Criticism to Deconstruction: The Reception of Structuralism and Post-Structuralism*. Chicago: University of Illinois, 1988.

Beyerlin, Walter. *Weisheitlich-kultische Heilsordnung: Studien zum 15. Psalm*. BibS(N) 9. Neukirchen-Vluyn: Neukirchener Verlag, 1985.

_____. *Weisheitliche Vergewisserung mit Bezug auf den Zionskult: Studien zum 125. Psalm*. OBO 68. Göttingen: Vandenhoeck & Ruprecht, 1985.

_____. *"Wir sind wie Traeumende": Studien zum 126. Psalm*. SBS 89. Stuttgart: Katholishes Bibelwerk, 1978.

Bietenhard, Hans. ὄνομα, ὀνομάζω, ἐπονομάζω, ψευδώνυμος, *Theological Dictionary of the New Testament*, ed. Gerhard Friedrich, trans. Geoffrey W. Bromiley, 5:242-83. Grand Rapids MI: Eerdmans, 1967.

Birch, Bruce C. "Tradition, Canon, and Biblical Theology." *HBT* 2 (1980): 113-25.

Bitzer, L. F. "The Rhetorical Situation." In *Rhetoric: A Tradition in Transition*, ed. W. R. Fisher, 247-60. Ann Arbor: University of Michigan, 1974.

Black, Edwin. *Rhetorical Criticism: A Study in Method*. Madison: University of Wisconsin Press, 1978.

Blenkinsopp, Joseph. "A New Kind of Introduction: Professor Childs's *Introduction to the Old Testament as Scripture*." *JSOT* 16 (1980): 24-27.

Bloom, Harold. *A Map of Misreading*. New York: Oxford University Press, 1975.

Boylan, Patrick. *The Psalms: A Study of the Vulgate in the Light of the Hebrew Text*. Dublin: M. H. Gill and Sons, 1920–1924.

Brockington, L. H. *The Hebrew Text of the Old Testament*. Oxford: Oxford University Press, 1973.

Brooks, Cleanth. "The Formalist Critics." *Kenyon Review* 13 (1951): 72-81.

Broyles, Craig C. *The Conflict of Faith and Experience in the Psalms: A Form-Critical and Theological Study*. JSOTSup 52. Sheffield: Sheffield Academic Press, 1989.

Brueggemann, Walter. *Abiding Astonishment: Psalms, Modernity, and the Making of History*. Literary Currents in Biblical Interpretation. Louisville: Westminster/John Knox Press, 1991.

_____. "Bounded by Obedience and Praise: The Psalms as Canon." *JSOT* 50 (1991): 63-92.

_____. "A Convergence in Recent Old Testament Theologies." *JSOT* 18 (1980): 2-18.

_____. "The Costly Loss of Lament." *JSOT* 36 (1986): 57-71.

_____. "Formfulness of Grief." *Int* 31 (1977): 263-75.

_____. "From Hurt to Joy, From Death to Life." *Int* 28 (1974): 3-19.

_____. *Israel's Praise: Doxology against Idolatry and Ideology*. Philadelphia: Fortress Press, 1988.

_____. *Praying the Psalms*. Winona MN: Saint Mary's Press/Christian Brothers Publications, 1982.

_____. "Psalms and the Life of Faith: A Suggested Typology of Function." *JSOT* 17 (1980): 3-32.

_____. "A Shape for Old Testament Theology. II. Embrace of Pain." *CBQ* 47 (1985): 395-415.

_____, and Hans Walter Wolff. *The Vitality of Old Testament Traditions*. Second ed. Atlanta: John Knox Press, 1982.

Buss, Martin J. "The Idea of Sitz im Leben—History and Critique." *ZAW* 90 (1978): 157-70.

_____. "The Study of Forms." In *Encounter with the Text: Form and History in the Hebrew Bible*, ed. Buss, 1-56. Semeia supplements. Philadelphia: Fortress Press; Missoula MT: Scholars Press, 1979.

Buttenwieser, Moses. *The Psalms Chronologically Treated with a New Translation*. Chicago: University of Chicago Press, 1938.

Cardenal, Ernesto. *Psalms*. New York: Crossroad, 1981.

Cartledge, T. W. "Conditional Vows in the Psalms of Lament: A New Approach to an Old Problem." In *The Listening Heart: Essays in Wisdom and the Psalms in Honor of Roland E. Murphy, O. Carm.*, ed. Kenneth G. Hoglund, Elizabeth F. Huwiler, Johnathan T. Glass, and Roger W. Lee. JSOTSup 58:77-94. Sheffield: Sheffield Academic Press, 1987.

Cazelles, Henri. "The Canonical Approach to Torah and Prophets." *JSOT* 16 (1980): 28-31.

Chatman, Seymour. *Story and Discourse: Narrative Structure in Fiction and Film*. Ithaca NY/London: Cornell University Press, 1978.

Childs, Brevard S. *Biblical Theology in Crisis*. Philadelphia: Westminster Press, 1970.

_____. *Biblical Theology of the Old and New Testaments*. Minneapolis: Augsburg/Fortress Press, 1993.

_____. *The Book of Exodus*. Old Testament Library. Philadelphia: Westminster Press, 1974.

_____. *Introduction to the Old Testament as Scripture*. Philadelphia: Fortress Press, 1979.

_____. *The New Testament as Canon: An Introduction*. Philadelphia: Fortress Press, 1984.

_____. *Old Testament Theology in a Canonical Context*. Philadelphia: Fortress Press, 1985.

_____. "Psalm Titles and Midrashic Exegesis." *JSS* 16 (1971): 137-50.

_____. "A Response." *HBT* 2 (1980): 199-211.

_____. "Response to Reviewers of *Introduction to the OT as Scripture*." *JSOT* 16 (1980): 52-60.

_____. Review of James A. Sanders, *Torah and Canon*. *Int* 27 (1973): 88-91.

_____. "The Exegetical Significance of Canon for the Study of the Old Testament." In *Congress Volume, Göttingen 1977*, 66-80. VTSup 29. Leiden: E. J. Brill, 1978.

Clements, Ronald E. *Abraham and David: Genesis 15 and Its Meaning for Israelite Tradition*. SBT 2nd ser. 5. London: SCM Press, 1967.

_____. *A Century of Old Testament Study*. London: Lutterworth, 1976. Revised ed. 1983.

_____. *Exodus*. CBC. Cambridge: Cambridge University Press, 1972.

_____. *God and Temple : The Presence of God in Israel's Worship*. Philadelphia: Fortress Press, 1965.

_____. "Patterns in the Prophetic Canon." In *Canon and Authority*, ed. G. W. Coats and B. O. Long, 42-55. Philadelphia: Westminster Press, 1977.

_____. "Temple and Land: A Significant Aspect of Israel's Worship." *TGUOS* 19 (1963): 16-28.

Clines, David J. A. *I, He, We, & They: A Literary Approach to Isaiah 53*. JSOTSup 1. Sheffield: JSOT Press, 1976.

_____. "The Parallelism of Greater Precision." In *Directions in Biblical Hebrew Poetry*, ed. Elaine R. Fallis. JSOTSup 40. Sheffield: JSOT Press, 1987.

_____. "Psalm Research Since 1955: II. The Literary Genres." *TynBul* 20 (1969): 105-25.

Clines, David J. A., David M. Gunn, and Alan J. Hauser, eds. *Art and Meaning: Rhetoric in Biblical Literature*. JSOTSup 19. Sheffield: JSOT Press, 1982.

Collins, Adela Yarbro, ed. *Feminist Perspectives on Biblical Scholarship*. Biblical Scholarship in North America. Chico CA: Scholars Press, 1985.

Collins, Terence. "Decoding the Psalms: A Structural Approach to the Psalter." *JSOT* 37 (1987): 41-60.

Craigie, Peter C. *Psalms 1-50*. WBC 19. Waco TX: Word Books, 1983.

Croatto, J. Severino. *Biblical Hermeneutics: Toward a Theory of Reading as the Production of Meaning*. Trans. Robert R. Barr. Maryknoll NY: Orbis, 1987.

Croft, Steven J. L. *The Identity of the Individual in the Psalms*. JSOTSup 44. Sheffield: JSOT Press, 1987.

Cross, Frank Moore, Jr. *Canaanite Myth and Hebrew Epic*. Cambridge MA: Harvard University Press, 1973.

Cross, Frank Moore, Jr., and David Noel Freedman. *Studies in Yahwistic Poetry*. SBLDS 21. Missoula MT: Scholars Press, 1975.

Crossan, John Dominic, ed. *Paul Ricoeur and Biblical Hermeneutics. Semeia* 4. Missoula MT: Scholars Press, 1975.

Culler, Jonathan. *Framing the Sign: Criticism and Its Institutions*. Oklahoma Project for Discourse and Theory. Norman OK/London: University of Oklahoma Press, 1988.

_____. *On Deconstruction: Theory and Criticism after Structuralism*. London: Routledge & Kegan Paul, 1983.

_____. *The Pursuit of Signs*. Ithaca NY: Cornell University Press, 1981.

_____. *Structuralist Poetics: Structuralism, Linguistics and the Study of Literature*. London: Routledge & Kegan Paul, 1975.

Culley, Robert C. *Oral Formulaic Language in the Biblical Psalms*. Near and Middle East Series 4. Toronto: University of Toronto Press, 1967.

_____. "Structural Analysis: Is it Done with Mirrors?" *Int* 28 (1974): 165-81.

Culpepper, R. Alan. *The Anatomy of the Fourth Gospel*. Philadelphia: Fortress Press, 1983.

_____. "Commentary on Biblical Narratives: Changing Paradigms." *Forum* 5 (1989): 87-102.

Dahood, Mitchell. *Psalms*. Three vols. AB 16, 17, 17A. Garden City NY: Doubleday, 1966–1970.

Darr, Katheryn Pfister. *Isaiah's Vision and the Family of God*. Literary Currents in Biblical Interpretation. Louisville: Westminster/John Knox Press, 1994.

Davidson, Robert, and A. R. C. Leaney. *Biblical Criticism*. Pelican Guide to Modern Theology 3. Hammondsworth: Penguin, 1970.

Davies, Eryl W. "Land: Its Rights and Privileges." In *The World of Ancient Israel*, ed. Ronald E. Clements, 349-69. Cambridge: Cambridge University Press, 1989.

Davis, Robert Con, and Ronald Schleifer, eds. *Contemporary Literary Criticism: Literary and Cultural Studies*. Second ed. Longman English and Humanities Series. New York: Longman, 1989.

Deissler, Alfons. *Die Psalmen*. Die Welt der Bibel. Düsseldorf: Patsmos-Verlag, 1963.

Delekat, Lienhard. *Asylie und Schutzorakel am Zionheiligtum*. Leiden: E. J. Brill, 1967.

Delitzsch, Franz. *Biblical Commentary on the Psalms*. Trans. David Eaton. London: Hodder & Stoughton, 1902.

Derrida, Jacques. "Différance." In *Margins of Philosophy*. Trans. Alan Bass. Chicago: University of Chicago Press, 1982.

_____. *Of Grammatology*. Trans. Gayatri Chakravorty Spivak. Baltimore/London: Johns Hopkins University Press, 1974.

_____. *The Post Card: From Socrates to Freud and Beyond*. Trans. Alan Bass. Chicago: University of Chicago Press, 1987.

Detweiler, Robert, ed. *Reader Response Approaches to Biblical and Secular Texts*. Semeia 31. Atlanta: Scholars Press, 1985.

_____. *Story, Sign, and Self: Phenomenology and Structuralism as Literary-Critical Methods*. Missoula MT: Scholars Press, 1978.

Eagleton, Terry. *Literary Theory: An Introduction*. Minneapolis: University of Minnesota Press, 1983.

Eaton, J. H. *Kingship and the Psalms*. SBT 2nd ser. 32. London: SCM Press, 1976. Second ed. The Biblical Seminar. Sheffield: JSOT Press, 1986.

_____. *Psalms*. Torch Bible Commentaries. London: SCM Press, 1967.

_____. "The Psalms and Israelite Worship." In *Tradition and Interpretation*, ed. G. W. Anderson, 238-73. Oxford: Oxford University Press, 1979.

Eco, Umberto. *The Role of the Reader: Explorations in the Semiotics of Texts.* Bloomington IN: Indiana University Press, 1979.

Eissfeldt, Otto. *The Old Testament: An Introduction.* New York: Harper & Row, 1965.

Eliot, T. S. *On Poetry and Poets.* London: Faber and Faber, 1957.

Exum, J. Cheryl, and David J. A. Clines, eds. *The New Literary Criticism and the Hebrew Bible.* JSOTSup 143. Sheffield: JSOT Press, 1993.

Fewell, Danna Nolan. *Circle of Sovereignty: Plotting Politics in the Book of Daniel.* Nashville: Abingdon Press, 1991.

_____. "Feminist Reading of the Hebrew Bible: Affirmation, Resistance, and Transformation." *JSOT* 39 (1987): 77-87.

Ficker, R. "רנן," *Theologisches Handwörterbuch zum Alten Testament,* ed. Ernst Jenni and Claus Westermann, 2:782-85. Munich: Chr. Kaiser Verlag; Zurich: Theologisches Verlag, 1979.

Fiorenza, Elizabeth Schüssler. *Bread Not Stone: The Challenge of Feminist Biblical Interpretation.* Boston: Beacon Press, 1984.

_____. *In Memory of Her: A Feminist Theological Reconstruction of Christian Origins.* New York: Crossroad, 1983.

Fisch, Harold. *Poetry with a Purpose: Biblical Poetics and Interpretation.* Bloomington/Indianapolis: University of Indiana Press, 1988.

Fish, Stanley. *Is There a Text in This Class? The Authority of Interpretive Communities.* Cambridge MA: Harvard University Press, 1982.

Fishbane, Michael. *Biblical Interpretation in Ancient Israel.* Oxford: Clarendon Press, 1984.

Fowl, Stephen E. "The Ethics of Interpretation or What's Left Over after the Elimination of Meaning." SBLSP 27 (1988): 69-81.

Freedman, David Noel. "Another Look at Biblical Hebrew Poetry." In *Directions in Biblical Hebrew Poetry,* ed. Elaine R. Follis, 11-28. JSOTSup 40. Sheffield: JSOT Press, 1987.

Frye, Northrop. *Anatomy of Criticism.* Princeton: Princeton University Press, 1957.

_____. *The Great Code: The Bible and Literature.* London: Routledge & Kegan Paul, 1982.

Funk, Robert W. *The Poetics of Biblical Narrative.* Sonoma CA: Polebridge, 1989.

Gamberoni, J. "חסה," *Theological Dictionary of the Old Testament* 5:64-75.

Geller, Stephen A. *Parallelism in Early Biblical Poetry.* HSM 20. Missoula MT: Scholars Press, 1979.

Gerstenberger, Erhard S. *Der Bittende Mensch: Bittritual und Klagelied des Einzelnen im Alten Testament.* WMANT 51. Neukirchen-Vluyn: Neukirchener Verlag, 1980.

_____. "פלל," *Theologisches Wörterbuch zum Alten Testament* 6, cols. 609-11.

_____. *Psalms: Part I with an Introduction to Cultic Poetry.* FOTL 14. Grand Rapids: Eerdmans, 1988.

Goldingay, John. "If Your Sins Are like Scarlet (Isaiah 1:18)." *Studia theologica* 35 (1981): 137-44.

Gorman, Frank H., Jr. *The Ideology of Ritual: Space, Time and Status in the Priestly Theology.* JSOTSup 91. Sheffield: Sheffield Academic Press, 1990.

Gottwald, Norman K. *The Hebrew Bible: A Socioliterary Introduction*. Philadelphia: Fortress Press, 1985.

Grant, Robert M., with David Tracy. *A Short History of the Interpretation of the
Bible*. Second ed. Philadelphia: Fortress Press, 1984.

Gray, George Buchanan. *The Forms of Hebrew Poetry*. 1915. Reprint, with intro.
by David Noel Freedman. New York: KTAV, 1972.

Greenberg, Moshe. "The Biblical Conception of Asylum." *JBL* 78 (1959): 125-
32.

Greenwood, David. "Rhetorical Criticism and *Formsgeschichte*: Some Methodological Considerations." *JBL* 89 (1970): 418-26.

Gunkel, Hermann. *Die Psalmen*. GHK 2. Göttingen: Vandenhoeck & Ruprecht,
1926.

_____. *The Psalms: A Form-Critical Introduction*. Facet Books, Biblical Series
19. Philadelphia: Fortress, 1967.

Gunkel, Hermann, and Joachim Begrich. *Einleitung in die Psalmen*. Göttingen:
Vandenhoeck & Ruprecht, 1933.

Gunn, David M. "New Directions in the Study of Biblical Hebrew Narrative."
JSOT 39 (1987): 73.

_____. *The Story of King David: Genre and Interpretation*. JSOTSup 6.
Sheffield: JSOT Press, 1978.

Haran, Menahem. *Temples and Temple-Service in Ancient Israel: An Inquiry into
the Character of Cult Phenomena and the Historical Setting of the Priestly
School*. Oxford: Oxford University Press, 1978.

Hasel, G. *Old Testament Theology: Basic Issues in the Current Debate*. Third ed.
Grand Rapids: Eerdmans, 1972.

Hayes, John H. *Old Testament Form Criticism*. San Antonio TX: Trinity
University Press, 1974.

_____, and F. Prussner. *Old Testament Theology: Its History and Development*.
Atlanta: John Knox Press, 1985.

Heinen, K. "Das Nomen tᵉfilla als Gattungsbezeichnung." *BZ* 17 (1973): 103-
105.

Hirsch, E. D., Jr. *The Aims of Interpretation*. Chicago: University of Chicago
Press, 1976.

_____. *Validity in Interpretation*. New Haven: Yale University Press, 1967.

Holland, Norman N. *5 Readers Reading*. New Haven: Yale University Press,
1975.

_____. *Poems in Persons: An Introduction to the Psychoanalysis of Literature*.
New York: W. W. Norton & Co., 1973.

House, Paul R. *Beyond Form Criticism: Essays in Old Testament Literary
Criticism*. Winona Lake IN: Eisenbrauns, 1992.

Iser, Wolfgang. *The Act of Reading: A Theory of Aesthetic Response*. Balti-
more/London: Johns Hopkins Univesity Press, 1978.

_____. *The Implied Reader: Patterns of Communication in Prose Fiction from
Bunyan to Beckett*. Baltimore: Johns Hopkins University Press, 1974.

_____. "Indeterminacy and the Reader's Response in Prose Fiction," in *Aspects
of Narrative*, ed. J. Hillis Miller, 1-45. English Institute Essays. New York:
Columbia University Press, 1971.

_____. "Interaction between Text and Reader." In *The Reader in the Text: Essays on Audience and Interpretation*, ed. Susan R. Suleiman and Inge Crosman. Princeton: Princeton University Press, 1980.

Jackson, Jared J., and Martin Kessler, eds. *Rhetorical Criticism: Essays in Honor of James Muilenburg*. PTMS 1. Pittsburgh: Pickwick Press, 1974.

Jacobson, Richard. "The Structuralists and the Bible," *Int* 28 (1974): 146-64.

Jemielity, Thomas. *Satire and the Hebrew Prophets*. Louisville: Westminster/John Knox Press, 1992.

Jenni, E. "עוֹלָם," *Theologisches Handwörterbuch zum Alten Testament* 2, cols. 228-43.

Johnson, Aubrey R. *The Cultic Prophet and Israel's Psalmody*. Cardiff: University of Wales Press, 1979.

_____. *Sacral Kingship in Ancient Israel*. Cardiff: University of Wales Press, 1955.

Keel, Othmar. *The Symbolism of the Biblical World: Ancient Near Eastern Iconography and the Book of Psalms*. Trans. Timothy J. Hallett. New York: Seabury, 1978.

Kennedy, George A. *New Testament Interpretation through Rhetorical Criticism*. Studies in Religion. Chapel Hill/London: University of North Carolina Press, 1984.

Kessler, Martin. "A Methodological Setting for Rhetorical Criticism." *Semitics* 4 (1974): 22-36.

Kikawada, Isaac M. "Some Proposals for the Definition of Rhetorical Criticism." *Semitics* 5 (1977): 67-91.

Kirkpatrick, A. F., ed. *The Book of Psalms*. CBSC. Cambridge: Cambridge University Press, 1902.

Kissane, Edward J. *The Book of the Psalms*. Volume 1. Dublin: Browne and Nolan, 1953.

Kittel, Bonnie. "Brevard Childs's Development of the Canonical Approach." *JSOT* 16 (1980): 2-11.

Knierim, Rolf P. "Old Testament Form Criticism Reconsidered." *Int* 27 (1973): 435-68.

Knight, Douglas A. "Canon and the History of Tradition: A Critique of Brevard S. Childs's *Introduction to the Old Testament as Scripture*." *HBT* 2 (1980): 127-49.

_____. "The Understanding of 'Sitz im Leben' in Form Criticism." SBLSP 1 (1974): 105-25.

Koch, Klaus. *The Book of Books: The Growth of the Biblical Tradition*. Trans. Margaret Kohl. Philadelphia: Westminster, 1968.

Kraeling, Emil G. *The Old Testament since the Reformation* New York: Harper & Row, 1955) 18.

Kraus, Hans-Joachim. *Psalms 60–150: A Commentary*. Trans. Hilton C. Oswald. Minneapolis: Augsburg/Fortress Press, 1989.

Kugel, James L. *The Idea of Biblical Poetry: Parallelism and Its History*. New Haven CT/London: Yale University Press, 1981).

Landes, George M. "The Canonical Approach to Introducing the Old Testament: Prodigy and Problems." *JSOT* 16 (1980): 32-39.

Lang, Bernhard, ed. *Anthropological Approaches to the Old Testament*. IRT 8. Philadelphia: Fortress Press, 1985.

Lentricchia, Frank. *After the New Criticism*. Chicago: University of Chicago Press, 1980.

Lewis, C. S. *An Experiment in Criticism*. Cambridge: Cambridge University Press, 1961.

Long, B. O. "Recent Field Studies in Oral Literature and Their Bearing on Old Testament Criticism." *VT* 26 (1976): 187-98.

_____. "Recent Field Studies in Oral Literature and the Question of *Sitz im Leben*." *Semeia* 5 (1976): 35-49.

Lowth, Robert (1710–1887). *Prælectiones de sacra poësi Hebræorum*. 1753. Trans. G. Gregory. 1787.

Macintosh, A. A. *The Psalms: A New Translation for Worship. Notes on the Text*. London: Collins Liturgical Publications, 1977.

Mailloux, Steven. *Interpretive Conventions: The Reader in the Study of American Fiction*. Ithaca NY/London: Cornell University Press, 1982.

Martin, Wallace. *Recent Theories of Narrative*. Ithaca NY/London: Cornell University Press, 1986.

Mays, James L. "What Is Written: A Response to Brevard Childs's *Introduction to the Old Testament as Scripture*." *HBT* 2 (1980): 151-63.

McCann, J. Clinton, ed. *The Shape and Shaping of the Psalter*. JSOTSup 159. Sheffield: Sheffield Academic Press, 1993.

_____. *A Theological Introduction to the Book of Psalms: The Psalms as Torah*. Nashville: Abingdon Press, 1993.

McCullough, W. Stewart, William R. Taylor, J. R. P. Sclater, Edwin McNeill Poteat, and Frank H. Ballard. "The Book of Psalms," *Interpreter's Bible* 4:1-763. New York/Nashville: Abingdon Press, 1955.

McEvenue, Sean E. "The Old Testament, Scripture or Theology?" *Int* 35 (1981): 229-42.

McFague, Sallie. *Metaphorical Theology: Models of God in Religious Language*. Philadelphia: Fortress, 1982.

_____. *Speaking in Parables: A Study in Metaphor and Theology*. Philadelphia: Fortress, 1975.

McKeating, H. "The Development of the Law on Homicide in Ancient Israel." *VT* 25 (1975): 53-56.

McKenzie, Steven L., and Stephen R. Haynes, eds. *To Each Its Own Meaning: An Introduction to Biblical Criticisms and Their Application*. Louisville: Westminster/John Knox Press, 1993.

McKnight, Edgar V. *The Bible and the Reader: An Introduction to Literary Criticism*. Philadelphia: Fortress Press, 1985.

_____. *Postmodern Use of the Bible: The Emergence of Reader-Oriented Criticism*. Nashville: Abingdon Press, 1988.

Melugin, R. F. "Muilenburg, Form Criticism, and Theological Exegesis." In *Encounter with the Text: Form and History in the Hebrew Bible*, ed. M. J. Buss, 91-102. *Semeia* supplements. Philadelphia: Fortress Press; Missoula MT: Scholars Press, 1979.

Meyers, Carol L. "Gender Imagery in the Song of Songs." *HAR* 10 (1987): 209-23.

Meyers, Carol L., and Michael O'Connor, eds., *The Word of the Lord Shall Go Forth*. Philadelphia: American Schools of Oriental Research, 1983.

Michel, Diethelm. *Tempora und Satzstellung in den Psalmen*. Abhandlungen zur Evangelischer Theologie 1. Bonn: H. Bouvier u. Co. Verlag, 1960.

Milgrom, J. "Sancta Contagion and Altar/City Asylum." In *Congress Volume, Vienna 1980*, 278-310. VTSup 32. Leiden: Brill, 1981.

Miller, D. A. *Narrative and its Discontents: Problems of Closure in the Traditional Novel*. Princeton: Princeton University Press, 1981.

Miller, Patrick D., Jr. *Interpreting the Psalms*. Philadelphia: Fortress Press, 1986.

_____. "Poetic Ambiguity and Balance in Psalm XV." *VT* 39 (1979): 416-24.

Miller, Patrick D., Jr., Paul D. Hanson, and S. Dean McBride, eds. *Ancient Israelite Religion*. Philadelphia: Fortress Press, 1987.

Miscall, Peter D. *1 Samuel: A Literary Reading*. Indiana Studies in Biblical Literature. Bloomington: Indiana University Press, 1986.

Molina, David Newton de, ed. *On Literary Intention*. Edinburgh: Edinburgh University Press, 1976.

Mosca, Paul. "Psalm 26: Poetic Structure and the Form-Critical Task." *CBQ* 47 (1985): 212-37.

Mowinckel, Sigmund. *The Psalms in Israel's Worship*. Two vols. Trans. D. R. Ap-Thomas. New York/Nashville: Abingdon Press, 1962.

Muilenburg, James. "Form Criticism and Beyond." *JBL* 88 (1969): 1-18.

_____. "The Linguistic and Rhetorical Usages of the Particle כי in the Old Testament." *HUCA* 32 (1963): 135-60.

_____. "A Study in Hebrew Rhetoric: Repetition and Style." In *Congress Volume*, 97-111. VTSup 1. Leiden: E. J. Brill, 1953.

Murphy, Roland E. "The Old Testament as Scripture." *JSOT* 16 (1980): 40-44.

Nicholson, E. W. *Deuteronomy and Tradition*. Philadelphia: Fortress Press, 1967.

Nicolsky, N. M. "Das Asylrecht in Israel." *ZAW* 48 (1930): 146-75.

Nida, Eugene A., Johannes P. Louw, A. H. Snyman, and J. v. W. Cronje. *Style and Discourse: With Special Reference to the Text of the Greek New Testament*. Cape Town: Bible Society, 1983.

Norris, Christopher. *Deconstruction: Theory and Practice*. New Accents. New York/London: Methuen & Co., 1982.

Noth, Martin. *The Deuteronomistic History*. JSOTSup 15. Sheffield: JSOT Press, 1981.

_____. *A History of Pentateuchal Traditions*. Trans. Bernhard W. Anderson. Engelwood Cliffs NJ: Prentice-Hall, 1972.

Oesterley, W. O. E. *The Psalms. Translated with Text-Critical and Exegetical Notes*. London: SPCK, 1939.

Ogden, G. S. "Psalm 60: Its Rhetoric, Form, and Function." *JSOT* 31 (1985): 83-94.

Parsons, Mikeal C. "Canonical Criticism." In *New Testament Criticism and Interpretation*, ed. David Black and David Dockery, 255-94. Grand Rapids: Zondervan, 1991.

_____. *The Departure of Jesus in Luke-Acts: The Ascension Narrative in Context*. JSNTSup 21. Sheffield: JSOT Press, 1987.

_____. "Reading a Beginning/Beginning a Reading: Tracing Literary Theory on Narrative Openings." In *How Gospels Begin*, ed. Dennis E. Smith, 11-31. *Semeia* 52. Atlanta: Scholars Press, 1990.

Patrick, Dale, and Allen Scult. *Rhetoric and Biblical Interpretation*. JSOTSup 82 and Bible and Literature series 26. Sheffield: Almond Press, 1990.

Perrin, Norman. "Historical Criticism, Literary Criticism and Hermeneutics." *JR* 52 (1972): 362-64.

Phillips, Gary A. "Exegesis as Critical Praxis: Reclaiming History and Text from a Postmodern Perspective." In *Poststructural Criticism and the Bible: Text/History/Discourse*, 7-49. *Semeia* 51. Atlanta: Scholars Press, 1990.

Pleins, J. David. *The Psalms: Songs of Tragedy, Hope, and Justice*. Maryknoll NY: Orbis Books, 1994.

Plottel, Jeanine Parisier. "Introduction." In *Intertextuality: New Perspectives in Criticism*, ed. Jeanine Parisier Plottel and Hanna Charney, xiv-xx. New York Literary Forum 2. New York: New York Literary Forum, 1978.

Polk, David P. "Brevard Childs's *Introduction to the Old Testament as Scripture*." *HBT* 2 (1980): 165-71.

Polzin, R. M. *Biblical Structuralism: Method and Subjectivity in the Study of Ancient Texts*. Philadelphia: Fortress Press, 1977.

Praeder, Susan Marie. "Jesus-Paul, Peter-Paul, and Jesus-Peter Parallelisms in Luke-Acts: A History of Reader-Response." SBLSP 23 (1984): 38-39.

Prince, Gerald. *Narratology: The Form and Functioning of Narratives*. New York: Mouton, 1982.

Rabinowitz, Peter J. *Before Reading: Narrative Conventions and the Politics of Interpretation*. Ithaca NY/London: Cornell University Press, 1987.

_____. "Truth in Fiction: A Reexamination of Audiences." *Critical Inquiry* 4 (1977): 121-41.

Rad, Gerhard von. *Old Testament Theology*. Volume 1. Trans. D. M. G. Stalker. New York: Harper & Row, 1962.

_____. *Studies in Deuteronomy*. SBT 9. London: SCM Press, 1953.

Rast, Walter E. *Tradition History and the Old Testament*. GBS. Philadelphia: Fortress, 1972.

Ray, William. *Literary Meaning: From Phenomenology to Deconstruction*. Oxford: Basil Blackwell, 1984.

Reventlow, H. *Problems in Old Testament Theology in the Twentieth Century*. Philadelphia: Fortress Press, 1985.

Richter, Wolfgang. *Exegese als Literaturwissenschaft: Entwurf einer alttestamentlichen Literatur Theorie und Methodologie*. Göttingen: Vandenhoeck & Ruprecht, 1971.

Ricoeur, Paul. *The Conflict of Interpretations: Essays in Hermeneutics*, ed. Don Ihde. Evanston: Northwestern University Press, 1974.

_____. *Essays on Biblical Interpretation*, ed. with an introduction by Lewis S. Mudge. London: SPCK, 1981.

_____. *Interpretation Theory: Discourse and the Surplus of Meaning*. Fort Worth: Texas Christian University Press, 1976.

_____. *Interpretation Theory and the Rule of Metaphor: Multidisciplinary Studies of the Creation of Meaning in Language*. Trans. Robert Czerny with Kathleen McLaughlin and John Costello. London: Routledge & Kegan Paul, 1978.

Riffaterre, Michael. *Semiotics of Poetry*. Advances in Semiotics. Bloomington/London: Indiana University Press, 1978.

Rimmon, Shlomith. *The Concept of Ambiguity—The Example of James*. Chicago: University of Chicago Press, 1977.

Rimmon-Kenan, Shlomith. *Narrative Fiction: Contemporary Poetics*. New Accents. London/New York: Methuen & Co., 1983.

Robertson, David. *The Old Testament and the Literary Critic*. GBS. Philadelphia: Fortress Press, 1977.

Rogerson, J. W., and J. W. McKay. *Psalms 51-100*. CBC. Cambridge: University Press, 1977.

Russell, Letty M., ed. *Feminist Interpretation of the Bible*. Philadelphia: Fortress Press, 1985.

Said, Edward W. *Beginnings: Intention and Method*. New York: Basic Books, 1975.

Sanders, James A. "Adaptable for Life: The Nature and Function of Canon." In *Magnalia Dei: The Mighty Acts of God. Essays on the Bible and Archaeology in Memory of G. Ernest Wright*, ed. Frank Moore Cross, Jr., Werner E. Lemke, and Patrick D. Miller, Jr., 531-60. Garden City NY: Doubleday, 1976.

_____. "Biblical Criticism and the Bible as Canon." *USQR* 32 (1977): 157-65.

_____. *Canon and Community: A Guide to Canonical Criticism*. GBS. Philadelphia: Fortress Press, 1984.

_____. "Canonical Context and Canonical Criticism." *HBT* 2 (1980): 173-97.

_____. *From Sacred Story to Sacred Text: Canon as Paradigm*. Philadelphia: Fortress Press, 1987.

_____. *Torah and Canon*. Philadelphia: Fortress Press, 1972.

Saussure, Ferdinand de. *Course in General Linguistics*, ed. Charles Bally and Albert Seceharge in collaboration with Albert Reidlinger, trans. Wade Baskin. New York: Philosophical Library, 1959.

Sawyer, John F. A. "An Analysis of the Context and Meaning of the Psalm-Headings." *TGUOS* 22 (1967–1968): 26-38.

_____. "Types of Prayer in the Old Testament." *Semitics* 7 (1980): 131-43.

Schmidt, Hans. *Die Psalmen*. HAT. Tübingen: J. C. B. Mohr [Paul Siebeck], 1934.

Schmidt, Werner H. *Old Testament Introduction*. Trans. Matthew J. O'Connell. New York: Crossroad, 1984.

Schwartz, Regina M. "Introduction: On Biblical Criticism." In *The Book and the Text: The Bible and Literary Theory*, 1-15. Oxford: Basil Blackwell, 1990.

Sheppard, Gerald T. "Canon Criticism: The Proposal of Brevard Childs and an Assessment for Evangelical Hermeneutics." *Studia Biblica et Theologica* 4 (1974): 3-17.

Silberman, Lou H., ed. *Orality, Aurality and Biblical Narrative. Semeia* 39. Atlanta: Scholars Press, 1987.

Smart, James D. *The Past, Present, and Future of Biblical Theology*. Philadelphia: Westminster Press, 1979.

Smend, Rudolf. "Questions About the Importance of the Canon in an Old Testament Introduction." *JSOT* 16 (1980): 45-51.

Smith, Barbara Herrnstein. *Poetic Closure: A Study of How Poems End.* Chicago: University of Chicago Press, 1968.

Spender, Stephen. "Remembering Eliot." In *T. S. Eliot: The Man and His Work,* ed. Allen Tate. New York: Delacorte Press, 1966.

Spivey, Robert A. "Structuralism and Biblical Studies: The Uninvited Guest." *Interpretation* 28 (1974): 133-45.

Steinmetz, David C. "The Superiority of Pre-Critical Exegesis." *Theology Today* 37 (1980): 27-38.

Stendahl, Krister. "Biblical Theology, Contemporary." *Interpreter's Dictionary of the Bible.* A-D: 418-32. New York/Nashville: Abingdon Press, 1962.

Sternberg, Meir. *The Poetics of Biblical Narrative: Ideological Literature and the Drama of Reading.* Indiana Studies in Biblical Literature. Bloomington: Indiana University Press, 1985.

Stout, Jeffrey. "What Is the Meaning of a Text?" *New Literary History* 14 (1982): 1-12.

Stuhmueller, Carroll. *Psalms 1 (Psalms 1-72).* OTM. Wilmington DE: Michael Glazier, 1983.

Sugirtharajah, R. S. ed. *Voices from the Margin: Interpreting the Bible in the Third World.* Maryknoll NY: Orbis Books, 1991.

Suleiman, Susan R., and Inge Crosman, eds., *The Reader in the Text: Essays on Audience and Interpretation.* Princeton NJ: Princeton University Press, 1980.

Tannehill, Robert C. "The Composition of Acts 3-5: Narrative Development and the Echo Effect." SBLSP 23 (1984): 238-40.

Tate, Marvin E. *Psalms 51-100.* WBC 20. Dallas: Word Books, 1990.

Tate, W. Randolph. *Biblical Interpretation: An Integrated Approach.* Peabody MA: Hendrickson, 1991.

Thomas, D. Winton. *The Text of the Revised Psalter.* London: SPCK, 1963.

Thompson, H. C. "The Right of Entry to the Temple in the Old Testament." *TGUOS* 21 (1965–1966): 25-34.

Tillyard, E. M. W., and C. S. Lewis, *The Personal Heresy: A Controversy.* London/New York/Toronto: Oxford University Press, 1939.

Todorov, Tzveton. "Reading as Construction." In *The Reader in the Text: Essays on Audience and Interpretation,* ed. Susan R. Suleiman and Inge Crosman. Princeton: Princeton University Press, 1980.

Tolbert, Mary Ann. *Sowing the Seed: Mark's World in Literary-Historical Perspective.* Minneapolis: Fortress Press, 1989.

Tompkins, Jane P., ed. *Reader-Response Criticism: From Formalism to Post-Structuralism.* Baltimore/London: Johns Hopkins University Press, 1980.

Torgovnick, Marianna. *Closure in the Novel.* Princeton: Princeton University Press, 1981.

Trible, Phyllis. *God and the Rhetoric of Sexuality.* OBT. Philadelphia: Fortress Press, 1978.

_____. *Texts of Terror: Literary-Feminist Readings of Biblical Narratives.* OBT. Philadelphia: Fortress Press, 1984.

Tucker, Gene M. *Form Criticism of the Old Testament.* GBS. Philadelphia: Fortress Press, 1971.

Uspensky, Boris. *A Poetics of Composition: The Structure of the Artistic Text and Typology of a Compositional Form*. Trans. Calentina Zavarin and Susan Wittig. Berkeley: University of California Press, 1973.

Vater, A. M. "Story Patterns for a *Sitz*: A Form- or Literary-Critical Concern?" *JSOT* 11 (1979): 47-56.

Wagner, N. E. "*Rinnah* in the Psalter." *VT* 10 (1960): 435-41.

Watson, Wilfred G. E. *Classical Hebrew Poetry: A Guide to its Techniques*. JSOTSup 26. Sheffield: JSOT Press, 1984.

Weiser, Artur. *The Psalms: A Commentary*. Old Testament Library. London: SCM Press; Philadelphia: Westminster, 1959.

Weiss, M. "Die Methode der 'Total-Interpretation'." *Congress Volume, Uppsala 1971*. VTSup 22: 88-112. Leiden: E. J. Brill, 1972.

_____. "Wege der neuen Dichtungswissenschaft in ihrer Auswendung auf die Psalmen Forschung." *Biblica* 42 (1961): 255-302.

Welleck, Rene, and Austin Warren. *Theory of Literature*. New York: Harcourt, Brace, and Co., 1942.

Westermann, Claus. *Elements of Old Testament Theology*. Trans. Douglas W. Stott. Atlanta: John Knox Press, 1982.

_____. *Praise and Lament in the Psalms*. Atlanta: John Knox Press, 1981.

_____. *The Psalms: Structure, Content & Message*. Trans. Ralph D. Gehrke. Minnneapolis: Augsburg, 1980.

_____. "Struktur und Geschichte der Klage im Alten Testament." *ZAW* 66 (1954): 44-80.

_____. *What Does the Old Testament Say about God?* ed. Friedemann W. Golka. Atlanta: John Knox Press, 1979.

Westermarck, Edward. "Asylum." *Encyclopedia of Religion and Ethics*, ed. James Hastings, 2:161-64. Edinburgh: T. & T. Clark, 1909.

Wilson, Gerald H. *The Editing of the Hebrew Psalter*. SBLDS 76. Chico CA: Scholars Press, 1985.

_____. "Evidence of Editorial Divisions in the Hebrew Psalter." *VT* 34 (1984): 337-52.

_____. "The Qumran Psalms Manuscripts and the Consecutive Arrangement of Psalms in the Hebrew Psalter." *CBQ* 45 (1983): 377-88.

_____. "The Use of Royal Psalms at the 'Seams' of the Hebrew Psalter." *JSOT* 35 (1986): 85-94.

Wimsatt, W. K., Jr. *The Verbal Icon: Studies in the Meaning of Poetry*. Reprint. London: Methuen & Co., 1970. (Lexington: University Press of Kentucky, 1954).

Wuellner, Wilhelm. "Where Is Rhetorical Criticism Taking Us?" *CBQ* 49 (1987): 448-63.

Author Index

A Hermeneutic of Curiosity and Readings of Psalm 61

Mercer University Press, Macon, Georgia 31210-3960.
Isbn 0-86554-464-6. MUP/H364.
Text and cover design, composition, and layout by Edd Rowell.
Camera-ready pages composed on a Gateway 2000
     (via WordPerfect 5.1/5.2) and printed on a LaserMaster 1000.
Text font: TimesNewRoman 11/13 and 10/12. Display font: Helvetica.
Printed and bound by BookCrafters, Fredericksburg, Virginia 22408.
     Via offset lithography on 60# Booktext Natural paper.
     Cased in .088 binder boards.
     Cloth: Roxite C 56548 (blue) vellum finish.
     Matte pigment 916 (gray).
     Stamped with gold foil S19.

HIEBERT LIBRARY

3 6877 00018 4118

BS
1450
61st
.B45
1995
39125s